A JUMBLE OF CRUMPLED PAPERS

A CHURCH KID'S JOURNEY FROM CONFIDENCE, TO QUESTIONING, TO CHRIST

AUSTIN NOLL

A Jumble of Crumpled Papers: A Church Kid's Journey from Confidence, to Questioning, to Christ by Austin Noll

Unless otherwise noted, scripture quotations are from The ESV® Bible (The Holy Bible, English Standard Version®), copyright © 2001 by Crossway, a publishing ministry of Good News Publishers. Used by permission. All rights reserved.

ISBNs:

9781734021066 (print)

9781734021073 (ebook)

Published by:

Wise Path Books

a division of To A Finish LLC

12407 N MoPac Expy #250

Austin, TX 78758

www.wisepathbooks.com

To any person
whose relationship with church or God
could most accurately be described
as a bit ... jumbled.

CONTENTS

PROLOGUE: THE BEGINNING
OF SOMETHING BEAUTIFUL

Here it is. The daunting first page of what I hope will be the beginning of something beautiful. Something bigger, better, and more impactful than anything I can conjure up in my head as I sit here writing it. For all I know, at this very moment, this book may not even become a reality. Right now, it is just an idea, or rather, a chaotic torrent of ideas wreaking havoc on my soul, begging to be told to someone, anyone, who will listen.

Obviously, if you are currently reading these words, it means that this book has indeed been written, and all of those ideas somehow miraculously found their way from my head, to my fingers, and onto enough pages to qualify it as a book. But right now, as I write these words, no such thing has yet happened. When I glance down, the rest of this page is blank. Empty. And all those ideas have yet to find their way out of my head. It's an overwhelming feeling, knowing all that I want to say. All that I *have* to say. And being aware of how much has to happen to get from where I am now as I write these words to where you are as you read them. So many questions and doubts and fears. But also excitement. Anticipation. Potential.

If you've found yourself in possession of this book, whether having come across it on the shelf of a bookstore or the bestseller's list on Amazon (a man can dream, right?), or perhaps having received it from a parent or your favorite aunt, you've probably read through the back cover or the table of contents and have a vague idea of what it's about. Maybe you haven't read anything and dove straight in cold turkey like an absolute psychopath. In either case, let me give you a quick rundown of what this book is about. In a few words... God. Church. Faith. Religion.

Now, depending on any number of factors and characteristics about yourself going into this, these words could invoke a spectrum of differing reactions. You might feel excitement, anticipation, eagerness. Perhaps you feel quite the opposite. Angry. Cynical. Hurt. Or maybe your disposition falls somewhere in between. Indifference. Ambivalence. Confusion even. And among all else, a feeling that I am confident traverses all of these... Questioning. We're human beings, after all. What else is our soul's deepest inclination when faced with the immensity that is the unknown than to question?

I write these words now, in a distant, yet just as equally intimate way talking directly to you because I myself have had these feelings toward these words and ideas. Which feelings, you ask? Well, to be frank... all of them. There have been distinct times in my life, many of which I can call to mind with pinpoint accuracy, where the idea of Christianity and church has filled me with joy, confidence, and purpose. And with just as little effort come to mind the times when those same ideas have been met with fear, doubt, guilt, shame, anger, even hatred. Right now, at this very moment,

I can say that there isn't one feeling listed above that I haven't felt about it all.

Now, the reasons for such reactions are, as you can guess, quite long-winded and difficult to communicate effectively without full context. So, for now, let me leave you with this. There is no right or wrong way to feel. No matter what anyone tells you, or what you may have grown up believing, any and every feeling you have toward the topics and ideas in this book are one hundred and twenty percent valid. This is because our feelings toward something are directly contrived from our experiences, and no experience is invalid.

As I wrestled with the idea of writing this book, I was confronted with the doubt of whether my experiences were really worth the time and effort it would take to tell them. Because, frankly, I love my life, and there is very little, if anything, that I would change. However, I believe that my experiences, both positive and negative, surrounding not just religion and church and God, but faith as a whole, are valuable in being able to help others gain a deeper understanding of their own beliefs and what they stand for. I can't invalidate my experiences, because if I do, I'll never be able to use them to help others.

No matter how much you may know about this book going in, I know you've at least read the title. And there is a high probability that you have absolutely no idea what it means. Good. After all, who doesn't like a good mystery? While I won't divulge the whole meaning of this concept right this very second, I will say this. Though our experiences, and the feelings accrued through them, are completely valid, there are many areas of our lives where how we feel toward something, or even someone, is based on faulty information.

For example, if you gave a person who has never before

tried fruit a lemon and told them it was a strawberry, they would believe that strawberries were incredibly sour and unpleasant to eat straight. Only once it is revealed to them that the sour fruit was in fact *not* a strawberry would they ever know that what they believed wasn't true. In their minds, based on what they were taught through their first-hand experience, they did not like strawberries. Only now do they realize that they were dealing with a completely different fruit altogether. How long can a person go without realizing a strawberry isn't a lemon?

This idea far transcends the differences in fruit, and is a familiar dynamic in many areas of our lives. Think about how many times just in this past week or month that you have realized that something you had believed was wrong, whether slightly or in its entirety. It happens *all the time*, with small things that hardly make a difference in our lives and things that may have been dictating a long-held mentality or how you conduct your life. Only once we are exposed to the correct information, or at least the complete information, can we actually decide how we truly feel about it.

While our feelings are always valid, they are not always accurate. You'd be surprised how many strawberries we have in our lives that we have come to believe are lemons. And because of that, we have succumbed to doing our best to try and make lemonade out of what is rather unpleasant by itself, when all this time we could be enjoying the sweetness of the strawberries just the way they are.

Let's get one thing straight right out of the gate. This book isn't going to give you all the answers. It won't fill in all the gaps, ease all the doubts, and tell you what to believe. This is my life. It is my experiences, my personal journey, and I will be sharing the things that I've learned and the understanding I've gained thus far. The truth is, in the grand spectrum of life, I'm still in the early stages, and the conclusions to most of the things I will discuss are still forthcoming. Just like you, I am in the midst of it. Learning as I go. One step at a time. And while I've undoubtedly already learned an invaluable amount in these first twenty-four years of my life, I know that in twenty-four years from now, I will be amazed at how little I know currently.

That is my hope. In fact, that is my goal, not just for me, but for you, which is a primary reason I am writing this. In the hope that, together, we can gain a deeper understanding of ourselves, God's desire for our lives and the way we live them, and how we can unearth the pure, raw, unadulterated truths that have, unfortunately, been so deeply buried in many areas of our faith that they have become mere shadows of themselves, rather than the foundations upon which we base so many of our convictions. The only way to truth is one step at a time. One page at a time.

Would you look at that? Five pages down already.

I'd say it's time to get started.

Wouldn't you?

(Note: Throughout this book, I discuss my experiences with churches and people from my own life. But the unfortunate truth is that this story isn't just mine. It is shared by many. As such, all names and identifying details have been removed or altered to retain the anonymity of those involved.)

PART I

IN THE BEGINNING...

1

BUILDING UP THE KINGDOM

I was six years old the first time I heard the voice of God. I don't know about you, but I don't remember a whole lot from when I was six. General things, sure. Vague, somewhat erased, and only half-constructed images of certain situations and interactions. Except for this moment. This moment I remember in vivid detail. My childhood bedroom was square shaped, and along one wall ran a shelf of cubicles holding my toys and various other belongings. There was a light fixture on the ceiling, the bulb encased in a large glass shade about the size of a soccer ball. And it just so happened that, if you were standing in front of the shelf, you would be directly under that light.

This is precisely where I found myself on this particular day, my lanky arms reaching into one of the cubicles trying to fish out a toy, when all of the sudden I had this... feeling. You could call it an awareness, a sensitivity, as if all of my senses had suddenly been dialed up a few notches. I stood frozen for a few fleeting seconds before I distinguished a voice in my head, telling me to press myself up against the shelf. Without any time to think it through, I listened, shuffling closer to the shelf, so that my toes were touching the bottom edge, the rest of my body leaning flat against it.

Within seconds, the glass light shade on the ceiling came crashing down, colliding with the hardwood floor and shattering to pieces right where I had just been standing. I don't remember much after that, probably due to the shock that I was experiencing at the whole situation. I had lived in that apartment my entire life up to that point, and that light had been there for just as long. It had never had any problems, and there was never any inclination that it was loose or posed any threat of danger. But at that moment, I didn't think about any of that. Within seconds, I had already concluded that I had just witnessed the intervention of God.

In fact, I never even considered any other alternative. Perhaps there was a flicker above me, just inside my peripheral vision, signaling to my senses that something was off. Or maybe a sound from the loose fixture kicked my reflexes into gear. I imagine if the same had happened to a child born into a home where God wasn't depicted as such a central force in the proceedings of the universe, they might have run through those possibilities first, and most likely come to a different conclusion altogether. But not me. I had been raised to equate the unprecedented with the supernatural, and taught that if I couldn't explain it, it was because God often works in unexplainable ways.

To be clear, I do believe this to be true in many facets of life, and I stand by the fact that God was indeed talking to me that day. However, it strikes me how quick I was, even at such a young age, to come to such an unquestioning explanation of what had happened. There wasn't a doubt in my mind that God had led me to move from underneath the soon-to-be falling light shade preemptively. I believed it was God, because I believed it couldn't have been anything else.

* * *

I was born into "the church." Let's start there. My parents were both actors, and moved to Los Angeles from different parts of the country to… well, act. Original right? They met for the first time at church shortly after moving to LA. My parents were a part of the early days of our church. In fact, my dad was our church's first official baptism over thirty years ago. They met, they fell in love, blah blah blah. Then their lives became a thousand times better when they had me.

In short, a life in the church was all I ever knew. From the time I could walk, my church's schedule was a core part of my life. The routine was deeply ingrained in me from a young age. Service every Sunday, small group in the middle of the week, Friday night devotionals during elementary, middle, and high school. Youth camps during the summer, Family Camp during the fall. If you have been a part of a church, you know the drill. I lived and breathed church because, honestly, church was the glue by which all other aspects of my life stuck together. And I thrived in it.

I consider myself a part of the Christian experience that I call "vanilla Christianity." And just to preface, no, this does not refer to the fact that I was one of the palest kids you have ever met, or that my church was one of those completely white congregations (One of the things that I quite admired about my church was how diverse it was. I was, however, unforgivably pale). It mainly serves to iterate the idea that the Christian lifestyle I grew up in was very ordinary, and even a bit plain. I grew up in a non-denominational church. If you aren't familiar with what exactly that means, here's a bit of a breakdown:

We weren't Anglican or Episcopalian because the only "bishop" we knew was the chess piece. We weren't

Methodist because no one on the worship team knew how to play the organ. We weren't Baptist because we much preferred contemporary music over hymns. We weren't Presbyterian or Lutheran because we believed you had to be baptized to be saved. We weren't Orthodox or Protestant because we believed that baptizing babies was even weirder than not being baptized at all. We weren't Catholic because none of us could speak Latin. And we weren't Pentecostal because, well, we weren't crazy. But really, I think the real reason we decided not to adhere to any traditional denomination is because we were all far too lazy to memorize and recite pre-written prayers.

We didn't meet in a traditional church building or chapel. We met at a high school. There were no pews or songbooks; we just stole songs from K-LOVE. We didn't have to dress up, and wore anything from the cliche plaid shirt and skinny jeans combo to graphic tees and basketball shorts. Most notably, there was very little austerity, no extreme or world-shattering beliefs or traditions that would put us on the hit lists of any other denominations or religions. We played it safe, kept to ourselves, and tried to stay out of the way. When asked what it means to be non-denominational, the answer was often that we "just follow the Bible." A satisfying enough response, don't you think?

But it wasn't just the church that catered to this "vanilla Christianity." A large part of it was my own life. I lived the stereotypical non-denominational American Christian life-style. I had a self-mandated fifteen-minute quiet time every morning before school. I felt guilty for any meal I consumed that wasn't prayed over beforehand. I not only never cussed, but took pride in being known as the kid who never did. In middle school, my wake-up alarm was Chris Tomlin's 2008 hit "God Of This City" (which quickly plummeted down my list of favorite Christian songs), and I listened to Casting

Crowns CDs in the car on the way to school (which have since remained at the top). I never had a girlfriend in middle and high school, not because I couldn't have if I had wanted (psshhh), but because I wanted to live as free from risk to my relationship with God as possible. In fact, I rarely ever hung out with a girl by myself at all.

I was the kid who would turn down going to a sports game, or a movie, or even a sleepover if it meant having to miss anything church-related. My nose was always buried in Christian books, as I was inspired to learn as much about God, and live as Christ-like a life as I possibly could. I also liked how all the finished books looked lined up on my shelf afterward. It gave off quite the image. I was homeschooled for the last three years of high school, sometimes taught by the pastor's wife and other ministry moms. I mean, you can't get much more vanilla than that.

I felt bad for all of the people around me who didn't go to church, especially when I was in traditional school, as I couldn't fathom what it would be like for it not to be a part of their life. What could you possibly be doing with all the extra time not spent attending Sunday service, midweek service, youth group, Bible talks, Bible studies, Youth Camp, Family Camp, worship concerts, summer festivals, and the occasional small group dinner? What else *was* there to do during those times?

If asked, many people would probably say that church is a part of their life. Not me. Church wasn't a *part* of my life. It was my life. And while God was definitely a contender, as I genuinely desired to have that relationship, church was unquestionably my defining factor. I found a large portion of my meaning in church. I felt pride in being someone who strived to live a life as closely connected to church and God as possible. I was one of the earliest of my friends to get baptized, and always thought of myself as one of the people whose stability in church would allow me to lead the way for those around me.

* * *

I was what many in our church would describe as a "Kingdom Kid," which is the term given to someone born into the church and whose parents are also Christians. They are children that grow up in the "Kingdom of God." In many ways, it is an unwarranted badge of honor worn by those deemed the most likely to stay faithful and become most valuable to the church and its mission once they grow up. You know how in school, at a certain age, the students who are more "gifted" in certain subjects get placed in advanced classes with more challenging curricula and expectant standards? It's a very similar dynamic with Kingdom Kids. However, unlike school kids who are better at math, Kingdom Kids usually aren't any different from their peers. The only difference is the perception that they are more stably grounded in the Church, and therefore have a greater potential to grow into the roles the Church desires for them to take on.

As you can imagine, growing up it was a very sticky dynamic for not only Kingdom Kids themselves, but the rest of their peers. For the people that didn't fit this characterization, whose families had come to church at a later stage in their lives, or perhaps were the only members of their family to attend, the hierarchy was clear to see. Even as kids, it was already easy to observe the emphasis placed on the Kingdom Kids. Although there was rarely any observably better treatment of the Kingdom Kids in opposition to everyone else, there was definitely a palpable *expectation* placed on them in how they acted and responded to what was presented to them in a faith setting. While those who were not Kingdom Kids were quickly written off if it seemed that their interest in God wasn't there yet, if a Kingdom Kid's investment in their spiritual life was lower than what was deemed the appropriate, "healthy" place to be, they would be bore down on to make sure they didn't stray from the path to their "spiritual success."

As I said, this structure was a detriment to both parties, those who were Kingdom Kids and those who weren't. For the people who weren't Kingdom Kids, it was clear from a very early age that their attainment of a thriving relationship with God just wasn't as important as those who were looked at as having a more assured place in the future of the Church. Growing up, I knew many friends who often felt like they had fallen through the cracks, were left behind and were allowed to just slip away. The thing that ends up being most hurtful is that when it happens, there is no sense of urgency from anyone to "pull them back up." It's as if they simply weren't viewed as important enough to invest the time or energy in setting them up for a thriving faith experience.

So many friends I grew up with felt put on the sidelines while the focus was on those who were already determined to live for Jesus and find their place in our church. In fact, there was a time in high school when all of the teen ministry students were placed in different small groups depending on where they were in their spiritual walks. Those who had already decided to follow Jesus met together, those who showed interest but were still seeking met together, and those who currently showed no interest, or were unsure of whether or not they wanted to follow Jesus at all, were in yet another group, completely secluded from everyone else. We weren't a large body of people, and everyone had close friends, sometimes even siblings, in different groups than their own. For those few years, the members of one group rarely got to see those of another on Friday nights when we met for small group devotionals, or whenever our small groups had other get-togethers.

Not only was it a terrible experience socially, but one of the saddest parts was that this system ruled out any possibility for crossover between those who had decided they wanted God and those who hadn't yet made that decision. If the problem isn't already apparent to you, let me help you out. How were you first introduced to God? Who were the ones who exemplified God's love and helped lead you to a deeper relationship with Him? The odds are it was either a family member or a friend.

Growing up, these people were family, even if not by blood. I had found myself to be in the group who had already decided they wanted to follow Jesus, but because we were all in the same group, there was rarely an opportunity for us to simply be around those who could probably benefit greatly from us just being around them and showing them how awesome Jesus is. Instead, all those with questions were put with others who had questions, and those who didn't want anything to do with God were grouped together with no friends to show them what God had to offer.

What these groups said about ourselves was no mystery to any of us. I was in the "best" group, and it still felt wrong. I can only imagine how those in the other groups felt, sanctioned off based on what I'm sure they were led to believe was the only valuable thing about them, which was how committed they were to God and the Church. Sure, each group was given lessons and taught about God, but right off the bat, we all knew exactly how important we were and how much our decisions actually mattered. In my group, we felt motivated and charged with empowering directive. In fact, the group of students who were Christ followers was aptly called the "Frontline," as in those who took up the front line in battle (Looking back, I now realize that usually in war, the people put in the front were the *least* valuable, but I guess they were still the ones to yell *"Chaaaaaaarge"* when the horns were blown. Maybe the point was that they were the most vigorous?).

The second group was appropriately called the "Seekers." Yet the last group didn't even get a name. Does the metaphor get any more painful? Not only did those in that group feel like the least important of everyone in our church's student body, but they weren't even given an identity. As if they were just... there. During this time, some of my closest friends were a part of this third group, and I can tell you that it wasn't because they didn't want anything to do with God. They just hadn't yet found where they fit in His story.

But back to the Kingdom Kids. The distinction of treatment between the different groups of people was clear, but the favor placed on those more "grounded" in Christianity definitely wasn't all favorable. Over the last few years, I have met and heard the stories of many people who grew up as Kingdom Kids, and one of the strongest similarities between their accounts was the feeling of having to "play the part." In an environment that placed a heavy expectation on the people brought up in it from birth, it was almost as if Kingdom Kids were predestined for the role the church desired for them. And when somebody found themselves not fitting that role as well as they were expected to, they often had to succumb and conform, even if their hearts were not in it.

I myself never felt that I ever had to play a part I didn't authentically feel I belonged in. Yet, this may have been because of how closely tied the structure of the church was to the overall structure of my life, in more ways than scheduling. It was my social epicenter. Yes, I had friends from other places. I was decently popular through school and always found my people. But my closest friends, the ones I considered my *real* friends, were from church. Why was this? For one, there was the moral aspect. I was aware that, generally speaking, my friends from church had a set of standards that not everyone held. And though, as kids and teenagers, what you believe fluctuates rather violently, there was an implicit expectation of how to conduct yourself and of what values you upheld as an individual and as a peer.

At times, this mindset impacted my intentionality with people outside of church. Somewhere in the back of my mind was the notion that the friendships I made in places other than my church wouldn't last, at least not nearly as long as those in my ministry. And to a degree, I was right. Many of my closest friends to this day are the ones I grew up with in church. Not only are they my longest-lasting friendships, but they are also the deepest. And it doesn't stop there. It's a generational thing.

Here's a prime example, and one that I share with people all the time. One of my best friends and I have known each other pretty much since the day we were born. Even before we were good friends, we were always around each other because our families were close way before either of us were born. Back in their single bachelor days, our dads were roommates in LA. This friend and I went to the same middle school, and continued to be best friends throughout high school and college. And then, like completely un-ironic clockwork, we too became roommates.

I could paint a very similar picture for many of my church friends. Really, the same could go for my entire age group at church. If you grew up in church then you know that the core age group you are introduced to when you start crawling is pretty much your ride-or-dies until the day you graduate high school. Every class, every event, every camp, they're your people, for better or for worse. We all had our ups and downs over the years, both individually and as a collective. But we really grew to know each other, even the ones we didn't necessarily hang out with all that much.

For me, church wasn't solely a Sunday venture. It was a foundational part of me. I'm sure if you got a very expensive microscope and inspected one of my DNA helixes, there would be a strand made up solely of those plastic-tasting communion wafers. And I wasn't just there for my friends. Sure, at a young age, most of us show up to see the people we know, and through the years, many continue to do so for the same reason. There's nothing wrong with that. I was in the same boat.

But there comes a certain time when you start to really think about why you're there. What do you believe? Could there be more here than just the social aspect? For those who didn't grow up in church, that line in the sand is quite distinctive. It's pretty easy to see the differences in lifestyle and beliefs of those in the church when you weren't born into it. However, that discovery requires a bit more intentionality for those who were. And once you begin bearing witness to the treasure buried beneath the surface, you begin to realize its value.

Once I realized that myself, I was in. All in. Bought in. Whatever other "in" phrase you can think of that means I was completely sold on not just the idea of God, and Jesus, and the Bible, but also the church itself. I was baptized when I was 14, which was the first truly intentional choice, made entirely on my own, to take that feeling and turn it into an action. And while baptism is a pledge of allegiance toward God, what I had yet to fully understand was that it is also, in many ways, a pledge of loyalty to the Church.

Whether this is good or bad, I cannot say. Ideally, this distinction wouldn't need to be made. In a perfect world, an allegiance to God *would be* an allegiance to the church, and vice versa. Two sides of the same coin. But, as I had at that time yet to learn, oftentimes, what is sanctioned by God and how it is lived by mankind are unfortunately less than identical.

My baptism was the first step in a long line of realizations and discoveries of the ways in which the many pillars of the Christian lifestyle, from personal convictions to churches themselves, have fallen so far short of what the Bible paints as God's true desire for our lives. Through my high school and college years, I have seen firsthand how young believers are being misled by churches, malnourished, and ultimately wrung dry of the true promises of God.

Though often well intentioned, the core foundational structures set forth by many churches for the lifestyle of young believers, due to their ultimate absence of God's most life-giving elements and characteristics, end up being detriments to their faith and sadly leave many with an incomplete, if not entirely inaccurate picture of who God is, as well as the true power of the Holy Spirit and His role in our lives.

In essence, this book will recount my experiences growing up in my church, the events that resulted in me eventually deciding to leave, and what I have learned since. To be clear, this will not be a "church bashing" dissertation on how the church is harmful to its members. Rather, I aim to help bring to light many of the untruths and uncertainties that plague the minds of many Christians, both young and old, and redirect you to the genuine truths that God sets for us as the standard for our relationship with Him.

I want to make something clear right away. I do not hate

the church. I owe many of my most valued relationships, memories, and beliefs to it. That being said, there comes a point wherein the harm being done sadly dilutes the good, resulting in a jagged and uneven faith experience that, if left untended, will most certainly cause, and already has caused, the desertion of faith altogether by so many people who truly desire God. In the end, I do not want to lead people away from the Church, but rather lend my hand in pointing out some of the problems that need fixing so that people will be led back not by fear or false expectation, but by the unequivocal feeling of the pure Gospel of God.

Untruth: *The Church is All Bad*
Truth: *The Church Can Be Better, Much Better*

2

THE NOTORIOUS C.C.C.

What is Christianity?

I know, I know. We're throwing around these types of questions in chapter *two?!* Don't worry, I'm not looking for the break-your-brain type of response. Depending on who you ask, you would probably get a spectrum of different answers, the most shared one likely being that Christianity is a religion, plain and simple. You may also get the occasional "It's not a *religion*, it's a *relationship*" quip from the ones who really want you to know that they're "one of the normal ones." And I think both answers are accurate. Of course, Christianity is by definition a religion. And being that it is founded on knowing Jesus, it would also inherently be relationship based.

But is this all that Christianity is? Is it *only* a religion? Is it just a relationship with Jesus? In a perfect world, perhaps it should be, though I am not the one to draw that conclusion. From my own experience and perspective, I can confidently say that Christianity has surpassed the classification of being solely a religion. It has evolved into a lifestyle, with its own universally distinguishable trends and characteristics. No longer is Christianity recognizable through beliefs and ideas alone. Nowadays, you can often tell that something or someone is "Christian" just by looking at them!

Christianity has a style. Whether or not that style is always *stylish* is up for debate. But there is definitely an indisputable "vibe" that is given off by things that are inherently Christian. And it's not subtle, with people of both religious and non-religious backgrounds often able to sense it from a mile away. It can be hard to explain, but I am confident you know what I'm talking about. Some things just reek of *Christian.*

On a purely foundational level, Christianity is, first and foremost, a religion. I don't think anyone would deny this. But I would argue that it has become something else in its own right that transcends religious rudiments and principles. Christianity has become a trademark. It has become a brand. It has become a *culture.* And a popular culture at that, with nearly seventy five percent of Americans considering themselves Christian. Does this mean they believe God sent His only Son to die for them and forgive them of their sins? I hope so. Does it mean that they have an active relationship with Jesus? Who can say. Sometimes those numbers make me wonder if perhaps so many people consider themselves Christians because they consider themselves partakers of Christian culture, whether or not it means adhering to its religious ideologies.

There are many branches to Christian culture, many facets that together lend themselves to what I like to call Contemporary Christian Culture, or CCC (oh yeah, it gets its own abbreviation and everything). In short, Contemporary Christian Culture is the cumulative collection of every custom, tradition, ideology, and the like that contemporary Christian churches adhere to and participate in. In other words, any particular church practice that, if explained to someone who isn't a Christian, they would think is absolutely insane and out of touch. Which, if we're being honest, is the case for many of them.

What ideas and practices fall under the ever-widening umbrella of CCC? Well, too many to fit in this chapter, I'll tell you that. I read a book not too long ago that was solely dedicated to all of these wacky, niche, and sometimes misunderstood things that only Christians do, aptly titled "Stuff Christians Like," which I highly recommend for some intriguing insight, if not just a genuinely good time. I think it's always good to take a step back and laugh at ourselves once in a while, and Christianity definitely has the material.

I'm sure we have all witnessed and lived examples of CCC in action. Depending on how long your Christian experience has been (or was), you may be more or less attuned to it than others. But often, it's impossible to miss. I'm talking about things like the intense advocacy of side hugs, as if the allowance of two people to commit to a full hug would surely end in one of them getting pregnant. Or worse. Catching feelings. I'm talking about the playful notion that the members of the worship team are just *slightly* more loved by Jesus than everybody else, even though that is so clearly false. Haha. Clearly. So totally and utterly clear. Mhm.

CCC puts a heavy focus on sharing your faith, which is not a bad thing at all. However, bring it to a younger crowd, such as high schoolers or college students, and the intensity gets kicked up thirty notches. You'd think they were training for the Evangelical Olympics, which includes the scariest event of all. Cold contact sharing. Which, if you aren't familiar, basically means walking up to a complete stranger and, within the span of thirty seconds, sharing your life story and trying to convince them that there is a void in their life that only Jesus can fill. I get chills just thinking about it.

CCC has been making strides in the world of Christian entertainment within the last decade or two. I know Christian music isn't for everyone, but personally, I'm a huge fan, while also acknowledging that a good portion of it tends to sound a lot alike. But we can all agree that the stuff being released now is leagues better than what churches had to work with twenty years ago. The same goes for Christian movies, although we still have our absolute cringe-fests, where the main character's pastor ends up solving the entire central conflict of the story by praying it away.

And let us not forget about the conferences! Conferences are like the new going-out-to-eat-with-friends. "Oh, you're coming to town next week? We should totally meet up and go to the North West East South Global Leaders of Serving, Discipleship, and 90 Day Prayer Conference together!"

Why bother paying five dollars for a cup of coffee when you can pay five *hundred* dollars and be able to drink *complimentary* coffee while a contender for that month's most influential celebrity pastor under thirty-five talks about how you, yes you, can be the one small spark your church needs to start a fire for the Lord and take your ministry to the NEXT LEVEL? We love our conferences. Maybe a little too much. But hey, on the plus side, they're a great place to find the person that God whispered to you in a dream will undoubtedly become your future spouse.

Speaking of future spouses, you think dating is difficult in the normal world? Wait till you try it in the world of CCC. With mixed signals running rampant, every leader wanting to have a say in your boundaries, and not a single person having the exact same idea how to go about it because it's not in the Bible, what can go wrong? A lot. A lot can go wrong. I think one of the reasons young Christians are getting married so fast is because they want to get in and out of the dating phase as quickly as possible to reduce the risk of anything going horribly wrong before they make it to the altar.

And maybe, just maybe, it has something to do with the wedding night. But that's a whole different conversation.

A significant tenet of CCC is its focus on serving, which comes directly from the core of Jesus's earthly ministry. From volunteering at food banks to helping at the local homeless shelter, Christians are far and away some of the most dedicated servers I've ever known. And while this all falls under the Christian culture tab, there is one aspect that smells a little more of that indistinguishable CCC aroma...

Mission trips.

Now, before you get upset, just let me explain. I've been on mission trips before. To far away lands. And they have been some of the most memorable experiences of my life. I specifically recall a ten-day trip to El Salvador, where my family and a group of church friends were able to dig a fresh water well for an impoverished local village. Real stuff. And awesome stuff.

But let's be honest here. Not all mission trips are like this. They aren't always, how would you say... *demanding*. While mission trips are always built around the opportunity to serve others, sometimes the resulting expedition ends up being just short of a glorified vacation, with a little bit of serving and a lot of awesome Instagram posts. While such a trip may not always result in a sunburned face and calloused hands, there will inevitably be a photo of a white church girl with their newly claimed African child plastered on their social media feed. Don't shoot the messenger. I don't make the rules.

I mentioned the style of Christian culture earlier, so let

me expand a little. The funny thing is, it doesn't matter when you read this book. I'm pretty confident these things will probably be nearly the same no matter how long it's been since writing it. Should we start with the plaid button-up, skinny jeans, beanie, and non-prescription glasses of a youth pastor's wardrobe, or the classic "I attend church" Christian woman outfit, including the short sleeve floral print dress, light wash denim jacket, mandatory wide brim fedora, and white sneakers? Contemporary Christian Culture is nothing if not predictable.

I could go on and on and on about the many aspects and tiny particulars of Contemporary Christian Culture. Growing up, I lived it every day. I was in deep. And I loved it. I absolutely loved the culture surrounding contemporary, first-world Christianity. I loved the weekend conferences held in four-star hotels. I loved the youth retreats and worship concerts and going to the bookstore and being able to choose between Bibles with hundreds of different styles and covers (The camo ones were the coolest, but I would always lose them...Badum tss).

I even loved Christian "tourist" fashion, as in the things you would wear if you took a trip to the official amusement park of Christ, including the cross-chain necklaces, Bible verse bracelets, and Christian t-shirts with funny puns. Being a fan of the tv show "The Walking Dead," I distinctly remember owning a shirt reading "The Son of God is Waking the Dead" in the same font and coloring as the show's title card. And I wore it with pride.

And of course, how could I forget the language? Along my descent to the deep end of the CCC pool, I also became well versed in Christian dialect. What's that? You didn't know Christianity had its own language? If you weren't already aware, let me tell you, yes, it does. Though we may not have our own alphabet or unique inflection, Christians hold their own collection of terms and jargon.

Referred to by many as "Christianese," sometimes it's commonly known words or phrases that we have endowed with an entirely new meaning, while other times it is completely made up altogether. Here are some of my favorite examples:

"**Worldly**"- Something that isn't "Godly", but is often used to describe anything that conflicts with someone's own personal beliefs, or that they just don't like.

Ex. *Have a good day at school, honey! And make sure to stay away from those worldly kids with the fake tattoos.*

"**A God Thing**"- Anything that happens without an obvious cause, whether it's actually because of God or not.

Ex. *I swear to you, Amazon said my package would be delivered in five to seven business days, but it got here in three! Totally a God thing!*

"**Wrestling**" or "**Struggling**"- Being completely and utterly steamrolled by whatever it is you are currently dealing with.

Ex. *If you all could pray for me, I've really been wrestling with gambling lately. On a totally unrelated note, does anyone have a spare bedroom for me, my wife, and my two kids? I kinda lost the house...*

"**Building**"- Growing a relationship with someone, usually with the intention of dating. Think of it as "pre-dating."

Ex. *Oh, I'm sorry. I'm not interested. I'm actually taken. Well, not* taken *taken, but we're building, so it's getting pretty serious.*

"Quiet Time"- An allotted amount of time dedicated to reading the Bible, praying, and connecting with God. Often used as an excuse just to get away from other people.

Ex. *Could you give me, like, fifteen minutes? The episode's almost ov- I mean... I'm having a quiet time.*

"I'll pray for you."- The odds of me praying for you are about 50/50, but hopefully the sentiment makes you feel good.

Ex. *I'll definitely be praying for you... Sharon? Steve. Right. I knew that. I'll definitely be praying for you Steve.*

"Lost"- Any non-believer/non-Christian. Sometimes even used to describe other Christians that simply do not go to *your* Church (more on this in a later chapter).

Ex. *Lastly God, I pray for all the Lost in the world, that they may find You. Especially all those over at Grace Cornerstone across town who went to the Metallica concert last weekend. Help them see Your truth, Father.*

"Check your heart"- I believe you are doing something incredibly wrong or stupid, but would rather you identify it yourself than have to point it out to you.

Ex. *You know, you may want to check your heart on that one. I mean, I'm not one to talk, but telling a girl that God told you she's going to be your wife minutes after she told you her favorite*

Bible verse is Ephesians 5:22-24 seems like something you may want to check your heart and pray about.

Over the last two decades, I have heard every one of these terms and phrases countless times and, guiltily, have used them all at one point or another. Just as Christians have specific things we do and ways we look, we also have many things we say that often only make contextual sense to other Christians. Sometimes it can be quite cool, feeling as if you're part of a super exclusive club with its own secret language and hidden meanings. But then you realize that, most of the time, those particular words and phrases don't make anything more straightforward, but usually cater to an unnecessarily complicated and exclusionary environment where what is said isn't always what is meant.

> **Untruth:** *Christianity Is Just A Religion*
> **Truth:** *Christianity Is A Culture*

* * *

One thing about Contemporary Christian Culture is that it's attractive. And one of the reasons it's so attractive is because it's comfortable. Where Christians in many parts of the world are met with intense persecution and violence for their faith, those of us in the United States can partake in the same beliefs and practices without any fear for our safety. Where being a Christian in other countries requires such a deep and intentional faith to have the courage to follow Christ, even when it means you could very well lose your life as a result, we can live in the culture of Christianity *for fun*, without even having to commit to any of the actual deep "religious aspects" of it if we don't want to.

Can you imagine someone in Nigeria, Libya, or Pakistan deciding to live a lifestyle of cultural Christianity just because it looked comfortable and easygoing, but not actually having any true conviction to want to follow Jesus? Their life would literally be on the line every single day. If you want to be a Christian in these and many other parts of the world, you have to really *want it*, enough to know the risk of what could happen to you, but still believe that Jesus is worth it. Yet, we can choose to be a part of Christianity simply because participating in the music on a Sunday morning makes us feel good.

Christian Culture is attractive to some people because it boasts the image of a well-put-together life. The common notion is that becoming a Christian makes us better people or enables us to get our lives in order and eliminate all of the negative parts holding us down. While that sounds nice, and in many cases people do appear to grow as Christians, it is not always because of the healing power of Jesus. While many facets of CCC are amusing, if not slightly contestable at their worst, other elements can, and do, inflict real, deep, and lasting harm on its members. Among them is the reality that CCC is a culture of perfection.

When I was growing up, there was a process that one was required to go through if they desired to get baptized in our church. They would need to be led through a series of curated Bible studies, where they would be taught the fundamentals of Christianity and Jesus. For what they provided, these studies did an adequate job of teaching us the information necessary to decide on getting baptized, while often falling short of providing the true heart and soul-level wealth that the good news offers.

However, if you were in youth group, from middle to high school, you usually weren't permitted to jump straight into the "core" Bible studies. First, you had to complete what were referred to as "character studies," which were about as on the nose as they sound. Once a week, a leader would lead you through a lesson focused on one particular aspect of your character, whether it be pride, honesty, obedience, humility, etc. They weren't always the same for each kid either. They were directly contrived from whatever aspects of their character the leader deemed they most needed to improve.

Basically, it was a weekly self-improvement course you were forced to go through if you wanted to become a Christian.

As if that alone wasn't bad enough, you were not allowed to advance to the subsequent character study until you proved that you were making progress on improving whatever part of yourself you were currently focusing on. And it was never based on how *you* felt you were doing. It was always up to whether or not the leader believed you were ready.

We literally had Jesus gate-kept from us by our own church. We started these studies because we genuinely desired to know and follow Jesus, yet we were told that we could only begin to do so once we worked on ourselves first. As if Jesus wouldn't accept us for who we were. And we believed it. We would spend weeks, months, being led through study after study working on ironing out all of our perceived character flaws while the cookie that was Jesus was being dangled right in front of us, always one step out of reach.

Many kids didn't make it through these character studies and ended up backing out before they were even given a taste of what they had come for in the first place, which was Jesus.

I always cringe when I remember my own studies when I was on track to getting baptized. I had to ask my friends about their accounts of the character studies for this book because I never got the chance to experience them myself. According to the leaders, when I was going to start my studies, I was "good" and could bypass the character studies and jump straight into the "real" studies.

Yikes. That makes quite the statement, doesn't it? And not about how good or put together I was. It was a flawed system, based solely on self-improvement and outward perfection while completely ignoring the basis for why someone would want to learn about Jesus in the first place. Countless numbers of young people, many who are my friends and peers, were taught that if they wanted to follow Jesus, they would have to meet Him halfway. Sure, He could help you with your problems and make you a better person, but you would first need to fix many of your biggest problems yourself.

I would be lying if I acted like this was some anomaly that only happened during this stage of our lives as believers. Whether or not anyone ever experienced a similar situation, we can go through our entire lives with a similar mindset. Once I was baptized, this dynamic was constantly present in nearly everything I did.

Every Sunday morning before service, the baptized high schoolers would split off by gender and have our discussion groups, which on paper were groups set to talk about life and help each other grow. This wasn't particularly *untrue*. But more often than not, each week when we convened, it would quickly digress into a session of Sin Management 101, going around the circle sharing what sins we had committed that week, figuring out ways to stop it, and move on to the next person.

Seldom did we ever discuss the idea that we are good, in the sense that, no matter what, God's got us. More often, the vibe was the need to white-knuckle and get a rein on all of the bad we were doing so that we could become better Christians. The entire church ecosystem was built around the pursuit of perfection and self-improvement, not on the power of God to change us from the inside out.

Contemporary Christian Culture, as a whole, shares very similar roots. Especially in those churches with younger crowds, who desire to do absolutely anything they can to get closer to God, that pure devotion is often molded into a step-by-step trudge through the mud of trying to "be better." It can feel extraordinarily validating and right for young people because it feels productive to try to improve yourself.

At least, when you see results. It's once we see that we are not achieving those results we desire when we begin to feel the weight of the expectations we are placing on ourselves. We seek perfection, but mask it as willful obedience to what God is calling us to do. But He doesn't want our perfection. He wants our heart.

This is not the only aspect of CCC that young people find attractive. Christianity, at its *core*, is not a culture. Really, it isn't even a religion (despite what I may have said earlier.) It is Christ. It is knowing and growing closer to Him. Everything else that Christianity is, all of its cultural styles and religious structures, should come directly from that core dedication to knowing Jesus, and helping others grow to know Him as well.

One of the primary methods that many contemporary churches are using to bring younger people to Jesus is through intense emotional experiences. One of the most attractive attributes of CCC is that it banks on emotion.

3

IT'S ALRIGHT TO CRY

It was a slower song.

They always played slower songs on that particular night.

I couldn't tell you what song it was, and I'm sure very few of the five hundred other kids in that amphitheater could tell you either. As I stood amidst the ocean of campers standing together and singing along, I knew that I wasn't the only one whose mind was anywhere but on the lyrics displayed on the screen. Though many of us were arm in arm, swaying back and forth in unison, others with their eyes closed, hands raised toward the sky, our thoughts were not on the song. Our thoughts were on what came after.

The third night of Teen Camp always felt colder than the rest, as if God wanted to mark the night distinctively by turning the thermostat of the San Bernardino mountains down a good fifteen degrees. It felt like this every year without fail. However, I quickly realized it was not the result of colder temperatures, but the unified nerves and anxiety of an entire camp of teenagers preparing to confess their sins.

Confession Night was a staple of the annual summer camp experience. Until my first year at Teen Camp, it was nothing short of legend, being spoken of in hushed tones and accompanied by furtive glances. "You think *this* is scary? Wait until Confession Night..."

The first year was the worst. As it turns out, sharing all of your most incriminating moral transgressions with a randomly selected group of people is NOT as fun as it sounds. But, as each year came and went, people came around to the idea that it wasn't so bad. Many even looked forward to it, as it was one of the year's most emotional and bonding nights. Plus, you didn't even need to spill the absolute worst things you'd ever done. You just had to share enough to convince people that what you were confessing *was* the worst stuff.

That was a joke, by the way. Unless you related to it...

In all seriousness, Confession Night was one of those things that we all just... did. We'd grown up hearing about it from older friends and adults and thought it was normal. It was a right of passage, signaling our graduation from childhood and entrance into the realm of maturity, where we could make our own choices and were ready for a real relationship with Jesus.

But who were we kidding? Who in their right mind, who didn't grow up in church, would agree to spend a whole night sharing the worst parts of themselves with a group of people they didn't even get to choose, which would sometimes be complete strangers? As Christians, we've been taught the benefits of confessing our sins to each other, but such a night as this would most often completely bewilder anybody else.

As my peers and I had simply grown up in it, Confession Night was a regular and expected part of our church camp experience. It made sense to have a night during camp when we could just get everything out, lay it before God and others, and continue on with a clear and unobstructed heart for the remainder of the week.

What it also became known for was the incredible worship night that took place afterward. Once everyone had completely spilled their guts, we would return to the amphitheater, dried tears on our faces, physically exhausted yet spiritually invigorated, completely and utterly emotionally vulnerable, and sing our heart out to a specifically chosen lineup of the songs that we had all come to know as the "heavy hitters." The songs that only came out during times like these. If you grew up in church, you know what I'm talking about.

Soon enough, tears would return to the recently dried eyes, campers would link arms and grab shoulders in a newfound unity born in the flames of confronting their inner demons, and the room would shake with the sound of hundreds of hoarse voices wailing every word until either the song ended or they passed out. It was often a toss-up between which would happen first.

I had known growing up that many churches had confession nights. What I didn't know is that oftentimes this night is referred to as "Cry Night." It wouldn't take a rocket scientist to deduce why. While these nights don't always involve full on confession groups, the intent is pretty much the same. Get everyone united, and give them the chance to confront themselves, whether wrongs they've committed, relationships they need to mend, or hurts to verbalize, and hopefully dedicate (or rededicate) their life to Jesus.

Now, there are some positive aspects of these nights, one of the main ones simply being to give people an allotted time to conduct the type of introspective work they would likely never get anywhere else, at any other point in their day-to-day lives. But something that always felt a bit off to me, which I was never quite able to pinpoint until years later, was how systematic it all felt.

After these nights at camp, I would feel better; there's no question. I felt lighter, closer to those in my group, and overall more connected to Jesus. Yet, at the same time, I couldn't shake the feeling that it was all somewhat... artificial. Manufactured. And though these nights personally left me in a better state, there was always a tiny part of me, at the very back of my mind, that felt manipulated.

* * *

During my recent delve online into the whole idea of Cry Nights, I happened across a Reddit post written by a former church camp attendee, who voiced a similar feeling about the way things were done, stating that it felt in a way like campers were being intentionally exhausted and emotionally spent so that they would be more susceptible to experiencing God, and hopefully deciding to follow Him.

This post validated that I may not be alone in my hunches. That was when I scrolled down and saw how many responses this post had, all from ex-youth campers and even a good number of former counselors and leaders, sharing much of the same. Despite the similarity in their accounts, it was shocking to read them all.

Here are just a few of the highlights:

"I experienced these nights as a camper every time, then as a camp counselor learned the intentionality of it. We discussed in meetings the way the camp week is orchestrated to lead to an emotional spiritual experience toward the end. It's all structured for that goal."

. . .

"The Thursday night. There was an intense, prolonged devotional. Dark hall, multitude of candles, emotional music, the works. It would be anticipated all week. It was clear that it was totally intentional. People cried, we wrote our sins on pieces of paper and burned them, would chant over and over along with the guitar, were encouraged to write letters to each other, tell our testimonies, there was a 'confessional' station which we felt pressured into going to (even if there was nothing to 'confess'). Of course there were then lots of images of Jesus on the cross, suffering for our sins. It was straight up psych manipulation. We were kids! Manipulated into feeling hatred and shame when we should have been enjoying our lives and identities!"

"I remember overhearing the worship team 'strategizing' on how to use lighting, repetitive songs (10 minutes of oh how he loves) and chord changes to lead into the salvation pitch. They were so aware of the fact that they got more results in the heightened emotional state than in a normal session. Most of the campers were only 10 years old!"

"I realized how blatant it was that they were using obviously not-spiritual things (low candlelight, emotional music, exhaustion, sappy letters from relatives...) to make us feel emotions that we would attribute to the Holy Spirit."

"When I was 17, I went to my first Jesus camp and it was awesome. I had so much fun. The final night, the resident band for that week played an original song they wrote and vamped the same chords over and over again for like half an hour and man I

thought it was beautiful. I thought about all my wrongdoings and problems in my life and I cried and 'became a Christian' again and it was magical. Even when I look back, it was a great night, but now I realize what led up to it. Exhaustion and manipulation. When kids started bursting into tears, they played softer and the pastor talked about forgiveness and born again Christianity and such and now I feel kinda duped that I fell for it. The Jesus camp 'high' wore off after about 3 weeks and I felt guilty and wondered why I only felt that way at camp. Good memories but I definitely feel tricked into crying and confessing due to tiredness and major sensory overload throughout the entire week."

"When I was in college (Christian liberal arts) I sat in on my roommate's class for students who wanted to be praise and worship leaders. The lecturer was literally explaining how they needed to study hypnosis practices to learn when to use certain songs to make people more emotional in certain parts of the church service."

"I worked as a counselor at a camp like this, though some sessions were markedly worse than others. They'd keep kids up late, run the Passion of the Christ brutality scenes in public places on loop, and have about 5 devos a day, including the late-night group therapy cry session. I loved so many things about that camp, but the browbeating and emotional warfare directed at kids in order to pressure them into baptism and self hatred was the worst part."

"I don't understand how they can even justify to themselves the use of psychological manipulation to emotionally overwhelm children and trick them into thinking they're having a spiritual reve-

lation. If your God is so great, you wouldn't need to rely on
trickery to get people to believe/reaffirm their faith."

In total, it took me over two hours to read through all of the
responses to the original post, *two hours* worth of people
sharing their stories about how they had first-hand experience with this emotional and spiritual manipulation being
dealt to adolescents, some as young as eight years old, all in
the name of trying to get them to dedicate their lives to
Jesus.

The intentional focus on heightened emotion during
Confession/Cry Night sets a false expectation of what it
looks like to be connected to God, equating authentic
connection with fabricated emotional provocation. I
remember, at times during those nights, looking around at
everyone singing their hearts out with tears in their eyes
and wondering if I was missing something essential because
I wasn't responding the same way. At other times, I was the
one singing my heart out because I "felt" connected to God,
when most of the time, it was just that I was emotionally
connected to what was happening around me.

There was an acknowledged connection between how
deeply a person was experiencing God and how expressive
they were of their emotions. Those who got caught up in
the passion around them were convinced it was because
they were being introduced face to face with Jesus, while
those who couldn't find that same enthusiasm questioned
the earnestness of their hearts. One of the trickiest parts is
that people can find themselves bouncing back and forth
between both sides of this equation simply depending on
how they are feeling at a particular moment. Usually, the
effects are felt most clearly once these emotional gatherings
are over.

* * *

There is a term that has become common for the phenomenon that can result from this dynamic, called the "Mountaintop Jesus." It is the idea that, because people have been taught that God's presence is most ostensibly experienced in these moments of intense emotional highs, they can begin to have a hard time finding Him anywhere else. He seems to be elusive in all of the ordinary, mundane parts of life, the valleys, and is only able to be found in the emotionally charged peaks of the mountaintops.

Some of the responses on Reddit shared similar impressions:

"Omg the GUILT I would feel after a week or so... losing that 'camp high' was my evidence that I wasn't trying hard enough and I needed to work harder, pray more, read my Bible and journal more to stay close to God. I was addicted. I went on every retreat, every mission trip, every summer camp, at least four per year from age 12-18. These camps, trips, and retreats all had the same emotional manipulation. I was constantly trying to recreate that feeling of intimacy, of being cared for, but no matter how hard I tried, away from the group I couldn't reproduce the same emotional response."

"I remember having so many guilt-filled chats with young campers about how they feel so 'close to God' at camp, but not as much at home and this would tear them up inside."

Every year when we went to camp, it was a widely shared expectation that upon coming home, the campers would be on what was often termed a "spiritual high." We had just spent a week away from civilization, away from our families, away from the internet and our phones and all of the noise, starved of sleep and quality food, and drowned in what could only be described as a tsunami of spiritual and emotional exorbitance.

While the bus ride up the mountain housed a mixture of excitement, nervous anticipation, and a hesitant indecisiveness shared among many of the kids regarding God and His role in their lives, the ride back down boasted an aura of exhausted, yet unyielding resoluteness and fire to live every second of every day for the glory of God. If experiencing God means feeling the way we felt at camp, why would anybody want to live any other way?

It was a running joke between my friends and me that so many kids would inquire about studying the Bible with a youth leader to get baptized upon returning from camp, only for eighty percent of them to lose steam and back out within the first month. So many of them would come back having felt things they had never quite felt before and told it came directly from God, that it *was* God. They were taught that being close to God meant continually living in a state of fierce emotional articulation, intimacy with those around you, and a unifying charge of purpose.

Little did they understand how inaccurate that picture would be for most of life. They were mistakenly sold the idea that those intentionally curated environments at camp, purposely set up for our emotional expression, were real life, and how a relationship with God is maintained.

But it doesn't last. It can't. As former youth camper and counselor Jen Bradbury writes in her article *Killing the Cry Night,* "While teens might- as I once did- temporarily associate those tears with feeling God, what happens when the camp high wears off? What happens to their faith when they're no longer in an artificial, carefully controlled environment? What happens when their tears dry and they get a good night's sleep? Too often, when that happens, teens feel as if they've lost God. They feel as though God is no longer with them. So, their faith starts to fade along with their memories of camp."

Every year, like clockwork, people would come back from camp with a tenacity and vigor I had never seen in them before, only for it to fizzle out within a few weeks, sometimes leaving them feeling more disheartened and isolated from God than before they left. In some cases, this cyclical letdown discourages them from wanting to pursue a relationship with God at all, while in others, the effects could be likened to a drug addiction.

I think about a heroin addict who, due to the high that comes from taking the drug, has become increasingly numb to anything that happens when they aren't. They crave their next hit, because only then can they actually feel. Just as one of our Redditor's responses explained, people become addicted to the spiritual and emotional highs achieved at places such as church camps because it is only in those moments that they truly feel connected to God. However, in reality, they have been blinded to the fact that God is just as reachable within the normalcy of life, and the effects of His presence often look and feel a lot different than a hoarse voice and tear-streaked face.

Don't think this idea applies only to church camp either. It translates to many aspects of Christianity, especially in our contemporary era.

Worship as a whole has been heavily impacted by the fixation on emotional reactions as a barometer for an individual's spiritual connection, as well as the Holy Spirit's presence among a congregation or gathering. From louder instruments to bigger screens to fancier lights with more movement and colors and fog machines to set the tone, churches are trying harder and harder to reach younger people through methods aimed at engaging their emotions.

I understand why. We live in a world where emotion is king, and a precedent has already been set of what a "good church" looks and feels like. Sadly, many of the churches that have developed this precedent have fallen into the same potholes of attracting millennials and Gen Z by providing them with very emotionally driven worship and sermon experiences.

Young people want to feel inspired, motivated, and set on fire with a cause they can throw themselves into whole-heartedly. They long for purpose and meaning. Yet, they don't always have the discernment, nor the patience, to see past the smoke and mirrors of what can initially seem like an enticing and fulfilling scratch to that itch.

The churches boasting those elements will be, and have been, the ones proving most successful in bringing in the next generation. And as other churches see "what works," they follow suit, bringing in the lights and the fog and what-ever else they need to show that they too can give these young people what they've been searching for.

And it may work for a while. But week after week, as people have come to expect that emotional high from their church experience, they are faced with the ever-steepening uphill climb of having to replicate it every week to match that same internal feeling. Regardless of how long they can keep it up, it quickly becomes fabricated and fake. It becomes a performance rather than humble, raw, unified worship of God.

I'm sure we all know churches like this, whether our own or one we've seen on tv or social media. So many contemporary churches, or churches *trying* to be contempo-rary, are compromising God's natural, all-encompassing presence for a forced and utterly unnatural imitation of it. As a result, their audiences, comprising mostly younger people, are being fed the same lie that God is found through emotion.

When you have been listening to music on max volume for years and years, turning it down to a normal level will sound empty and lacking. The same applies to the search for God. After being conditioned to believe that He is closest in the loudest room, people who attempt to seek Him anywhere else will undoubtedly be disappointed if they are not made aware of the distinction.

The moments where we are most emotionally charged are the times when we are also most open to making life-changing decisions. This is true of adults, and even truer among young people, which is no mystery to anybody, including those leaders of churches and counselors of camps. I honestly do not believe that most of these people have hostile intentions in how they implement and focus on these emotionally-evocative conditions. In most cases, they genuinely want to help young people find Jesus; for the most part, many simply do what they learned when they went through it themselves.

There are places for these elevated experiences, as truth can be found in our emotions. But that does not mean that the pursuit of emotion will result in the discovery of truth. It cannot become a staple of what it takes to achieve a relationship with God. This doesn't mean that God is not present in those moments, but it cannot take away from the fact that God is just as present in all of the ordinary, mundane parts of life. In fact, those may often be the places where He shines the brightest.

Untruth: *Emotion = Authentic Connection to Jesus*
Truth: *Authentic Connection to Jesus Is Expressed
In Many Different Ways*

4

THE WORLD BEYOND THE
WALLS

Since middle school, one of my favorite television shows
has been *The Walking Dead*. If you know the show, then you
probably know the premise: the undead have taken over the
world, and the survivors try to, well, survive. Though the
actual plot goes much deeper, with all kinds of character
arcs and narrative twists and turns, that is the general overarching idea. Survival. No matter the cost.

The show has been running for twelve years, and since
the very beginning, the characters have almost always been
fighting for a similar cause: finding somewhere they can be
safe. Over the span of eleven seasons, they have found
several such places, all with their own people, rules, and
ecosystems.

Throughout the course of the show, some of these "safe
havens" have withstood the test of time and zombies, while
many of the rest end up succumbing to their apocalyptic
adversaries and falling, leaving our group of survivors back
on the trek to find a new place to call home. However,
despite their distinctions, these communities share one

universal principle that all are strongly advised to follow. *If you want to live, stay inside the walls.*

For a religion founded on the promises of salvation and eternal life, Christianity seems to be a lot about surviving. As if, despite our shared belief that "no weapon forged against us shall prevail," we are somehow always on the brink of complete annihilation, and any association with things outside the walls of our spiritual safe haven will undoubtedly lead to our untimely demise.

From my earliest memories of church, there was always an aura of this sentiment, this trepidatious assurance, as if we had all made it onto the life raft just as the boat sank beneath the waters, yet if the raft were to overturn, we would still freeze or drown. We were safe, but only so long as we didn't make enough commotion to flip the raft.

As a young person in the church, it was a commonality to be constantly preached at about all of the things Christians ought not do or be a part of. It was consistently drilled into our minds that we shouldn't swear, shouldn't lie, shouldn't drink or smoke, shouldn't have sex before marriage, or talk to girls past ten o'clock for that matter, shouldn't listen to "bad" music or watch "bad" shows or movies, the list goes on and on and on. In reality, we probably spent more time being told all the areas of life that we couldn't participate in than all of the parts of life that are made incalculably better and we *are able to* experience because of God.

All of these "things" that we were told fell outside the circle of what constituted a Christian life were illustrated to us as being part of "the world." The outside world. The secular world. The anti-Christian world. The world whose inhabitants, for all intents and purposes, were going to end up in Hell.

Just like in *The Walking Dead*, we were taught that we were living in the apocalypse, but luckily had found ourselves in a community with towering walls and impenetrable gates. To remain inside the walls and adhere to the way things were done would mean to be guaranteed a life of security and prosperity. But if we were ever to transcend the protection of those walls, we were on our own in a world against us.

We would be on "The Outside," a barren wasteland with nothing to offer, but that would take everything from us. A place where not a single good thing exists, only evil; no matter how hard you try to withstand them, they will tear you away from God limb by limb. Of course, the vocalization may not have been that explicit. Yet the message was still strongly received. Though the world may look enticing, it was all a lie, and nothing outside God and the Church had any value for us. The only thing living in the world would do was destroy our relationship with God.

As Christian youth, we were encouraged by some church leaders to have as little contact with the outside world as possible. When we had to (many of us went to public school, were on sports teams, or other extracurriculars that were not church-related), we were fed as much negating information as possible to reduce the chances of us becoming "a part" of those worlds.

Have you ever seen what happens when a dandelion is submerged in water? It's like a bubble is placed around it, so even when put entirely underwater, it is still completely dry when it comes back out. That was the goal; to be "in the world, but not of it." To make sure, even in those instances where we had to be in the world, we would be completely unaffected by it.

I never questioned this, nor did those around me, as there was merit to what we were being told. There is a nobility to certain aspects of this perspective, as there is a lot of junk in this world. *A lot.* We all know many things are available to us that are better off left alone, and when we are taught which things to pursue and which to stay away from, it can really benefit us. But an issue that often presents itself is when things are painted as being objectively wrong, when in reality, that may not entirely be the case.

The Bible has a lot to say about what we should and shouldn't do, and the course of action is easier to discern for many of those things that are talked about directly. Yet, there are just as many things that the Bible says nothing about, at least in a direct manner, and in such cases, we are left to make those discernments ourselves.

For adults, those decisions are often left to their own discretion. But for kids and teenagers, the stick drawing the line between right and wrong was usually held by our church leaders. It wasn't our job to make those judgments since we didn't yet have the spiritual understanding or maturity to do so. But it was our job to listen to what we were being taught about the rights and wrongs of the world, and stay on our side of that line in the sand.

It sounds like a simple enough undertaking, to be taught what is right and wrong and strive to do the former. This is how young people are brought up in every area of life, so what's so different about it in a spiritual context?

My first answer to that question is that the ramifications implied by either doing the right or wrong thing are astronomically higher under a religious framework. If you cheat on a test instead of being honest about your ability, you may get sent to detention for an hour. But getting caught up in a lifestyle that causes you to lose sight of God? Well, you may very well be sent to Hell for eternity.

We were dealing with very real, everlasting conse-quences when it came to our decisions as church kids. And if it wasn't always the immediate threat of being denied access to Heaven, it was the constant pressure of keeping in good standing with our church, youth group, leaders, and peers. It was these disincentives, in no fixed order, that compelled us to try our hardest to comply with and obey every regulation administered to us.

It wasn't as if we were going against what we felt was right, as we believed that what we were being told regarding what was good or bad was, in fact, true. In many cases, it was. But as the years went on and we got older, signs started emerging that perhaps these principles weren't completely faultless, one of the most prominent being the ever-shrinking circle of spiritual approval.

Initially, I saw Christianity as a vast landscape that I was allowed to traverse any way I wanted, so long as I abided by the rules set forth which allowed me to do so safely. But as time passed, and my "Christian knowledge" increased and deepened, the list of do's and don'ts grew as well. With each new tenet of my faith that I was exposed to also came new restrictions and regulations, and slowly, that vast expanse began to shrink when in theory, it should have been expanding.

For a long time, it was just ideas and aspects of life that I had been taught believers were expected to have a particular viewpoint on. We believed this was the right way to go about this specific topic; thus, doing anything contrary would be going against that belief.

But soon enough, I realized that this also included people.

Just as "the world" comprised bad ideas and actions that could lead me away from God, so too did it have people who posed just as great of a threat to me and my faith. If they weren't a Christian, didn't know God, and didn't go to church, they would always be a negative force in my life.

Our youth ministry would often have talks about the importance of building our faith so that instead of being pulled down by those who aren't Christians, we could pull them up to our level. On the surface, this sounds admirable, and did to us when we heard it. But the fact that it was implied that every single non-Christian would be actively pulling us away from God if we didn't continually fight to grow our faith was a silent assassin, instilling in us, often unconsciously, the idea that the only people we could truly trust to build us up were our church and the believers around us.

Then one of my friends left our church. And it shocked me how quickly these ideas were expanded to include them as well. They had been a part of our church for years, since we were practically babies. They had been taught all the same things I had, chosen to be baptized like so many in our group, and yet, all of a sudden, they too were a threat to my relationship with God. Not due to any particular falling out of faith or denouncement of Jesus, but simply because they had decided to leave. That was when I began seeing where the line in the sand had truly been drawn.

One thing I had witnessed for years but had never really understood was that when a Christian from another church came to ours, even if they had been a believer all their life, they were usually required to re-study the Bible and get re-baptized.

It had never occurred to me, until this point, that it all catered to one singular belief. A large majority of us believed that we were the one true Church. I realized then that it wasn't about Christian and non-Christian things. It had never been solely about that. It had always been the belief that our church had the definitive truth, and everything we did and believed came from that definitive truth. Thus, anyone who believed anything differently than us was intrinsically wrong and was a threat to our inerrant faith.

It wasn't about people not believing in God. It was about people not believing in *our* God. Every viewpoint, perspective, and belief we had flowed from that foundational conviction. The walled safe haven that I had envisioned from childhood as being Christianity as a whole was in reality only my particular church, and what I was being kept shielded from was not solely Satan or The World, but any idea that conflicted with our own, which inherently included a world full of other Christians.

A quick Google search informs us that there are over two hundred denominations of Christianity in the U.S. alone, and a staggering forty-five *thousand* denominations globally. How we have managed to come up with forty-five thousand different interpretations of the Bible is beyond me. In any case, the question I pose is this: Are we so arrogantly confident in our specific views of God and the Bible that we don't believe that a single one of these forty-five thousand different perspectives has anything to offer us in our overall depiction of God?

I can say for a fact that every single denomination is wrong about something. I can safely bet that we are all wrong about multiple things, even many things. But to assume that not one of them has gotten something *right* that we may have missed is to declare that we have figured out God. Not only that, but we have also successfully confined Him to one particular sect of theology and culture.

The amount of sheer irreverence in such a notion astounds me. The amount of arrogance necessary to believe that God has deemed us worthy enough to reveal Himself in His fullness to us alone simultaneously sickens me and makes me laugh. The day we believe that we have God fully figured out is the day we should realize we have never been farther away on our quest to do so. I am embarrassed to have been involved with a community whose actions flowed from such narcissistic confidence.

Our belief that we have the incontestably correct picture of God is not only a discourtesy to Him, but also a monumental disservice to ourselves and our faith, for two reasons. One, it presents us with such an unimaginably smaller picture of God than what He desires for us to know, and smaller than we require to get through life. If our view of God is complete, there is a ceiling to what we can discover and understand, and thus a cap to the power we can obtain and utilize.

Every single person who has ever lived has believed in a smaller picture of God than who He actually is. This is because in order to comprehend God at all, we have to rationalize Him through our own human lens. Otherwise, we simply wouldn't be able to make sense of Him at all. But in doing so, we inadvertently confine God to our own ability to understand.

We know this, and there is nothing we can do about it except admit that we will never have the whole picture. That awareness enables us to continually seek, discover, and experience more of Him in different ways, allowing His effect on our lives to be more significant and profound. If we cannot do this, the god that we have will simply not be strong enough to handle our problems. And if God can't help us, there is no hope, as He *is* our hope.

The second reason is that if nobody has anything to offer, and everyone who has differing viewpoints to us is a threat, our world can quickly become suffocatingly small. Going back to the idea of a shrinking circle, being the gamer that I am, my mind unapologetically goes to a specific type of video game called a *Battle Royale*. If you're younger or more in touch with entertainment and pop culture, you might be familiar with this genre of game. If not, let me give you a basic rundown of how it works.

At the beginning of a match, one hundred players drop into a huge map, with the single goal of being the last man standing. Because of the sheer size of the battleground, a ring of death surrounds the map; in some games made of toxic gas; in others a storm or the like. As the game progresses and players are eliminated, this ring slowly closes in, decreasing the available play space and forcing the remaining players in a fixed direction, until at the very end, the last few players fighting are enclosed in an extremely small portion of the original landscape. If one steps outside this ring of available play space, they will begin to lose health, and if they don't return to the circle, they will eventually be killed.

Why do I bother explaining the details of a video game in a church book? Well, to be honest, not many other people tend to listen to me for very long when I try to do it in person. But also, it is uncannily reminiscent of what Christianity can become when we believe everyone else is wrong. No longer are we living in a unified life among other believers who are all experiencing God in different ways, being able to partake in their versions and depictions of God as we all share in them together. Instead, we are all fighting to be the last church standing in a game of Christian Battle Royale.

Instead of seeking knowledge and communion with others, we seek to indoctrinate them into our specific way of thinking. Instead of opening our doors to people with new ideas, we commit to a Mexican standoff-style confrontation. We stare them in the eyes, unflinching, our hands hovering above the holsters of our beliefs, nervously waiting for our opponent to flinch so we can unload onto them before they have the chance to blast their worldly and ungodly ideas at us. It doesn't matter whether we end up converting them or killing them, as long as their dangerous ideas are extinguished before they can lead any of our people astray.

We spend our time going from one fight to the next, all the while failing to notice the steadily encroaching ring of death, slowly engulfing the world around us. As it gets closer, we migrate with the ever-shrinking circle of safe space, perhaps even believing that the narrowing of our world is simply God weeding out the wrongdoers and the heretics. We move, and move, and move, fighting for our faith all the way, unflinching in the face of controversy and disparity, until, at last, we find ourselves in a circle no bigger than our own church, standing back to back, some on one leg, trying to balance off one another so as not to fall out of the circle into the ring of death that surrounds us. For at this point, everything outside our own four walls has been deemed a wasteland of the astray, and would surely only result in our destruction and desolation.

Is it even necessary to say that this is not the kind of life God desires for us? I doubt any person envisions this scenario and finds it compelling. I'm sure some have experienced something similar. When this is the lifestyle we lead, the faith that we preach, and the rules we put in place, we are not making followers of Christ. We are making followers of our specific ways of thinking, no matter to what extent Christ may be present in them.

* * *

There is a common phenomenon, which I have witnessed myself, that happens once church kids graduate high school and go off to college. Simply put, they have no clue how to handle themselves.

After eighteen years of being told that there is no other way to live life than as a Christian in their specific church, they are suddenly thrust out into the real world and find themselves face to face with the other 99.999% of life. They are exposed to ideas, beliefs, cultures, lifestyles, and people that they have perhaps never before had to deal with, at least on their own, with nobody telling them what they should or should not believe about them.

It's overwhelming, the clash of so many different ways of living and thinking. To go from an environment where everything is black and white, and certainty is declared adamantly, to practically drowning in an ocean of gray, where they have unrestrained power to observe, inspect, discern, and doubt anything and everything around them, is a shock unlike any other.

To their surprise, what they often find is not the wasteland of evil and danger they had been brought up believing would beat them into confusion and blind them to God. It is a seemingly infinite expanse of wonder and enlightenment, revealing to them just how vast and all-encompassing God actually is.

How do they handle it? Well, sometimes, understandably, this results in a crisis of faith. Everything they thought they knew about God and the world is suddenly condensed to a square cardboard box in a room stacked floor to ceiling with other boxes of all shapes, sizes, and colors. Having left home believing there was one proper way to live, only to discover that every single person around them does life a bit differently, views God a bit differently, and *seeks* God a bit differently, places them at the podium under the spotlight and forces them to decide what they are going to do about it.

Many simply don't have the capacity to deal with it. They get slammed by the tidal wave of new ideas, tossed back and forth by the turbulent waters, and spat out on the shore, exhausted, choking on water, and half dead. Their head is spinning, and they find themselves completely lost, having almost no idea where they are, or even *who* they are.

Depending on the person, they may lie there in the sand for a day, a week, a year, or many years. Some feel angry, deceived. They begin to question their entire spiritual disposition and where they belong in this very big world.

Many feel gypped, like they have been intentionally deprived of real life and fed a fairy tale instead. And it doesn't take long for them to see right through the facade, shove their Bible in a drawer, and set off in search of something new, something real.

In the end, some end up coming back to Christianity because, after making their rounds among many other alluring, yet ultimately empty paths, they conclude that Christ is in fact what their soul longs for.

Others never leave in the first place, but seek to integrate the small world of their upbringing with the grand discoveries of this new, larger world. Yet many never come back, because they spent years committed to a cause that has since been revealed to them as being only a tiny part of the whole picture, and convinced that they were the beholders of the only truth life has to offer, only to discover that there was so much more out there.

They were told they had all of God, and if what they had wasn't fulfilling enough, it was their fault. They weren't completely satisfied because they weren't praying enough. They weren't serving enough. They weren't devoted enough. They didn't believe enough. Their faith wasn't deep enough. And after years and years of being forced to believe it, they finally discovered that there *was* so much more of

God that they didn't have. And it wasn't their fault. These people don't return because their faith did not treat them with the respect they believe they deserve. And they are not wrong.

For decades, many Christian communities have raised their youth to believe that if they are not protected from all the bad in the world, they will most certainly end up succumbing to it. So they draw a line in the sand, stating that one side is good and safe, and the other is bad and dangerous.

Further, we hold the inaccurate assumption that God's presence is undeniably most attainable within the confines of our spiritual community. For that reason, we impart the notion to our youth that the world beyond our walls is deprived of God entirely. This is usually done out of a genuine desire to protect our loved ones from what we deem unnecessary hurt and an illusion of what is good and right.

But at some point or another, everyone enters the real world. It's an inevitability of life. And when we do, one of the most damaging things that can happen is realizing that it is nothing like how we were taught.

The world can be a dark and dangerous place. I think we all know that. The brokenness and godlessness of humanity is presented on full display every day. Yet where humanity falls short, God's sovereignty and grace often shines in a blinding fashion. There is simply too much of God in the world to attempt to compartmentalize him to the Church alone. By doing so, we are sending the message that we value people's fidelity to God to such an extent that we will compromise how much of Him they actually experience to ensure it.

Yet even though we may believe this will increase the chances of them staying faithful, more often than not, it results in the opposite. In the end, their desertion of faith wasn't caused by the dangerous and controversial ideas, beliefs, or people of the world. It resulted from the actions taken to sequester them from experiencing them.

We must teach people, especially young people, that there *is* more than one way to live. Rather than teaching that a life of God and church is the only way, we need to start sharing that it is not, but instead instill in them what that type of life has to *offer*.

> *"Train up a child in the way he should go; even*
> *when he is old he will not depart from it."*
> (Proverbs 22:6)

We are not in danger.

The Church is not in danger.

God is not in danger.

The biggest threat to the spiritual well-being of our children, friends, and loved ones is not the world. It is the harm done when our allegiance to God and the Church is outwardly expressed through acts not of faith, but of fear.

Don't get it wrong. Sometimes it can be very easy to be convinced that we are living in the apocalypse. It can be easy to shut our gates, fortify our walls, and close ourselves off to the rest of the world in an effort to safeguard what we hold most dear. But it is only when we allow ourselves to venture beyond those walls that we are able to see they weren't protecting us from death. They were hindering us from experiencing life to the full.

> **Untruth:** *The Outside World Is Devoid of God*
> **Truth:** *God Is Much Bigger Than Our Inside*
> *World*

PART II

THE FEAR FACTOR

5

THE FRAGILITY OF FEAR

Fun fact: Did you know that our being told to "fear not" is the most repeated command in all of the Bible? In fact, I've heard that the phrase is issued precisely 365 times, one reminder to not be afraid for every day of the year. Coincidence? Maybe. But I think we all know better than to think God coincidental.

Fear. AKA the number one greatest obstacle to our faith. As a matter of fact, I would argue that fear is in and of itself the exact *opposite* of faith. However, curiously, both terms revolve around one core characteristic.

Belief.

While faith is defined as the complete trust and confidence in something or someone, a belief that something is *good*, fear is regarded as the belief that something is dangerous, harmful, or has the potential to cause pain. The difference between these terms is not simply belief and the lack thereof, but how your belief is defined and what that belief is centered in.

* * *

Fear is many things.

It is misleading. It is divisive. Many would even consider it toxic. But above all of these, fear is destructive.

From the more personal aspects of one's confidence and self-esteem to its larger effects on communities and nations, fear is the uneven ground on which deceived empires are erected, only to crumble to dust by their own inert design. Wars may be won and lost by the amount of land conquered and lives taken, but if an army can impose fear on its enemies, these battles are over in the soldiers' hearts long before the killing blow is struck.

The same goes for literally any area of life that involves conflict or contestation. In sports, the team able to overcome the fear of their opposition will almost always arise on top, not nearly as dependent on their actual skill as you might think. I'm sure everyone has experienced the adverse outcomes of decisions grounded in fear at many points in their life. Missed opportunities that fester in your mind, sometimes for years. If you visit an elderly patient on the verge of passing and ask them what their biggest regret was, what they say will almost always be rooted in a decision made, or more often not made, because of fear.

Fear destroys all types of relationships, from marriages to dating couples to families and friendships. Lies are told out of fear of what the truth may reveal. Fear destroys futures. How many stories have been told, books written, films made, and songs sung about people who missed some of the biggest opportunities of their lives due to their own fear?

A wise man named Will Smith (Yes, that Will Smith) once said that God places the best things in life on the other side of fear. This statement couldn't be more true. Every single thing in life worth achieving is beyond the fear mounted against it. This fear is not impassable. But we cannot do it alone.

Jesus speaks on this in Isaiah 41:13 when He explains, "For I, the Lord your God, hold your right hand; It is I who say to you, 'Fear not, I am the one who helps you.'" The Bible iterates over and over how the biggest blessings awaiting you will not be delivered to your doorstep but are waiting for you across an ocean you can only cross if you hold onto God's hand.

Apart from a connection with God, a "fueling," if you will, you will not be able to overcome the things He has placed in your path solely for the purpose of Him being able to help you through. It was intentionally designed this way; Obstacles that are very clearly larger than our own ability to overcome, but easily overcome-able through a source of power that we ourselves do not contain.

Why?

So that there is no earthly way we can get to where we want to be, where we *genuinely* want to be, without God. We can try. Oh boy, do we try. But whether it takes days, or weeks, for some years and others whole lifetimes, God hopes that through our continued failures, we will eventually realize that *we can't do it alone*. Once we see that and take our eyes off the towering obstacles in front of us, God will be waiting right around the corner for us to turn to Him for help.

Notice the distinction I made between what we want and what we truly want. This is because, for many of us, what we think we want and what will actually bring everlasting satisfaction to our souls are very different things. That doesn't mean the things we strive for in our lives are bad. Most often, they are just simply too small.

Once we realize that this life was not meant to be gone through alone, but with a far superior being at our side directing and empowering each step we take, suddenly, the threshold of what is possible widens significantly, the ceiling of what we believed doable lifted infinitely. Then, when we are afforded the courage to dare to dream a little bigger, God reveals to us the true desires of our hearts and equips us with every tool needed to chase them.

How does this tie into fear? The answer is pretty simple, and rather blunt:

If fear dictates your life, you will experience none of this.

Let me say that again. If you allow fear to be your driving force instead of faith in God, you will experience *none* of the soul-fulfilling wonders God has in store for you.

And let me make sure this is clear as well. *Feeling* fear is an entirely different thing than *living in* fear. We all feel fear, every single day. They are fleeting nods, thoughts that come and go at a rapid rate. You may feel fear before a job interview, or a test, or a serious conversation with somebody.

Satan tempts us with fear at every possible interval throughout our day. But that is all he can do. Tempt us. He cannot force our hand in anything, but he sure can make it look appealing. When you decide to grab onto one of those fleeting fears, it will begin directing your steps, making you just a tad more vulnerable to the next temptation to be afraid that is thrown your way.

* * *

Imagine a suit of armor covering your entire body. These temptations to fear come as arrows, tiny and rather insignificant against your full body shield. Now imagine you decide to make just the tiniest hole in that armor. Most of your body is still protected, but there is that *one small space* where an arrow, if shot at just the right trajectory and speed, will sink right into you and take hold. Every time we agree to a small, relatively insignificant amount of fear, we add another hole to our armor, making us all the more vulnerable to the next shot.

Fear is an agreement, an intentional decision you make about how you perceive the world around you, and as such, it takes the same amount of intentionality to annul the effects. Every arrow that hits flesh stays there indefinitely until you willfully decide to grab it and pull it out. Meaning, if you continue to allow the slowly mounting number of fears to take hold and refuse to reject and remove them, you will soon be weighed down by hundreds of arrows sunken into your body.

If you had that many arrows stuck in you, how do you think that would affect how you lived? How you approach and tackle every single task in your everyday life? It would be much different, as you would be taking every step with extreme caution, afraid that if you let your foot down on the wrong piece of ground, or at the wrong angle, or perhaps even just a tad too hard, you would be filled with pain as those arrows wreaked havoc on your body.

I think you get the picture. Fear makes us fragile. But faith makes us firm. The more fear you give into, the more distracted you will be by the overwhelming implications of the arrows already piercing your body that you won't even be able to think about pulling any of them out. It is disabling, debilitating, and blinding. Your sole focus will be on surviving by any means necessary, when all God wants is for you to see that by pulling those arrows out and rejecting the ideas they represent, you will no longer just be surviving. You will be thriving.

Untruth: *Fear Keeps Us Safe*
Truth: *Fear Makes Us Fragile*

There is a place beyond fear where God wants to show us the wonders of life, creation, and Himself. We are capable of so little on our own. However, one of the few things *in* our control is our response to fear. Will we take it on, or will we disregard it as a lie, knowing that God's armor surrounds us? That is up to you, and it isn't a one-time decision. It is a conscious state of mind every day. The more we can discern this, and see through the lies of fear, the more of God we will be able to see and experience.

This is the goal and God's greatest hope for mankind. That we may seek Him, and perhaps reach out for Him (Acts 17:27), and in doing so, He may reveal to us the fullness of life, rather than the scraps that those who are enslaved to fear are left to scavenge. It is the path of every believer to find their way in this endeavor, growing in their knowledge and understanding of God and the Bible and thus growing closer to Him, and clinging to their growing faith in the face of all fears and insecurities so that God will pull them through and beyond.

As human beings, we are imperfect creations. We are perfectly made, make no mistake, but to intentionally be imperfect. Thus, we don't always see the direction God is calling us. We lose our way. Constantly. There are countless moments in our lives, every single day, where we fall short and lose sight of where God is and where He is calling us to go. And in those moments when we are in the dark and can't figure out which way is forward and which way is back, Satan is always there with a bow in his hands, and a quiver strapped to his back, ready to send the next arrow our way.

* * *

As a church, a body of imperfect believers, the members of a congregation are connected in many ways. Thus, when people find themselves in moments of fear, it can affect those around them.

This is natural and happens the most in circles of people who are most closely bonded. It's life, and in those moments, we are called to build one another up (1 Thess. 5:11) and help each other through our struggles.

But, as I have said and will continue to emphasize, we are imperfect. And there are many times when we fail to rise to the occasion. As a result, fears are left unresolved and turn to confusion. Confusion leads to misguidance. And the decisions made when misguided, if left unchecked and unrestrained, can create unhealthy roots that burrow deep into the foundation of believers' lives and spread like a virus until, before you've even realized it, they have permeated it and become strongholds in a church community.

I know for a fact that I am not alone in my church experiences, in which many of said strongholds were built up and rooted deep over years and years of unbridled and unresolved fears. People coming from rigid religious backgrounds are a commonality. People have been hurt by their churches, by spiritual leaders, and by friends in the faith. Many have turned away from their faith altogether as a result, and from an onlooker's perspective, it is, in many cases, completely understandable.

No church is perfect. That can be stated with confidence. There are many sermons, books, and the like on the topic of people continually getting mad at their churches and leaving in search of "the one," where their problems seem to fade away, and everyone is perfect. But every church has problems, and that is okay. In fact, that is beneficial, as problems are simply opportunities to grow, both individually and as a larger community. The issue is what happens when certain problems, which have taken the form of these more deeply rooted strongholds, aren't shown any effort to be fixed or are simply unrecognized or disregarded as less significant than they are.

When dealing specifically with young Christians, the doctrine of their church has a monumental effect on their own personal beliefs and opinions. Most of the time, they have blind faith in what their church presents as the path to salvation and a thriving relationship with God. Not until they are older and receive the life experience and perspectives of others outside of their church do they realize that sometimes, certain things they have been taught don't add up.

That, or, as is also common, something happens to them in their church, which, through seeking an answer to their questions, they are introduced to ideas that turn out not to be as healthy as initially believed. In almost all cases, these unhealthy ideas and questionable approaches to one's walk with God are rooted in fear.

6

THE S WORD

Are you familiar with the idea of "Chumra?" If you are accustomed to Jewish tradition, perhaps you have heard this term before.

The word itself simply means "stringency." In the context of Jewish religious discipline, the idea of Chumra relates to a more stringent practice of the Halakha than necessary. "Halakha" can be translated as "The Way" and is the term for the collective body of Jewish religious laws set in place to protect and preserve adherence to the Torah. In essence, Chumra is a way in which those who follow Jewish standards do so through much more severe methods than necessary in order to eliminate any possibility of transgression or infringement on the laws outlined in the Halakha. In other words, they go above and beyond what is actually commanded of them by Jewish law out of a fear of making any mistakes.

The rationale behind such a notion comes from a verse in Deuteronomy, the last book in the Torah. Verse 22:8 states that when one builds a house, they should build a parapet (or small wall or fence) around the roof to avoid the potential guilt of someone falling off. Many interpret this as a command to build a metaphorical fence around the Torah itself, which has led to countless such restrictions that are several degrees separated from the actual risk they are attempting to reduce.

One of the apparent drawbacks of this mentality is that it is tough to tell what is the actual Law of Moses and what is simply a Chumra that has been put in place by somebody else. Many young Jewish students are given restrictions exhorted as indisputable religious commands that in actuality are only Chumras set by Jewish leaders rather than scripture.

According to the accounts of some Jewish leaders and teachers, it has become a significant turnoff for young people, as they are being told that everything is forbidden without clarifying the basis of the prohibition. In effect, it makes these students want to abandon Judaism altogether.

Sound familiar? This brings to mind a similar experience during my senior year of high school, which continued well into college.

Though most people get their driver's license sometime during high school, or perhaps in college, the time when new drivers get their first car widely varies. By the end of high school, a select percentage of my friends had cars, while the rest didn't. At the time, I was borrowing my mom's minivan when needed.

Because of this, I was a valuable individual among my friends, and would often be the chauffeur for events and get-togethers, from going to the movies to going to lunch, and everything in between, including those meetups of our church's youth ministry. It eventually reached the point where I was considered the "soccer mom" of my friend group. Sometimes my mom's eight-seat minivan would be filled with ten people (don't ask me how), while at other times, it would just be me giving one other friend a lift. Being that our ministry comprised both guys and girls, naturally, there were times when I would be in the car alone with a girl.

In most situations, this would be considered entirely normal because, well, it is. There is no inherent problem with a guy and girl being alone in a car together. Especially if they are friends, and especially if they are mature, trustworthy individuals. To my knowledge, there was never any incident during my time in my church's youth ministry, and at any time before or since, incited by a guy and girl riding in a car together.

Yet, despite the lack of any causal incident, it was declared during a random Friday night teen devotional that, from that point forward, the only time a guy and a girl should ever be in a car alone together is if they are on their way to church or devo.

Now, as I said, included on the long list of destinations that my ride-share took were youth group devotionals and the occasional Sunday service. But these people weren't strangers. They were my friends, many of whom I had known for years and years. Our relationships weren't solely rooted in our attendance at church events; I had friends who were girls, just as I had friends who were guys.

To suddenly impose on us the idea that we were, in a way, prohibited from being in a car alone with someone of the opposite gender unless we were going to church not only put a roadblock in any genuine friendships between guys and girls but also implemented an idea that will come up more than once in this book, which is the promoting of a lack of confidence and trust in oneself. Clearly, our ministry leaders didn't trust us to be alone with someone of the opposite gender, so maybe we shouldn't either.

All of my friends saw the ludicrousness of this directive.

Yet, although I may not have agreed with what was being expressed, from then on, the aura when in a car with friends was less confident. Especially at the end of the day, as I dropped my friends off one by one, and the numbers started to dwindle, as it became clear that the remaining two people in the car would be of opposing genders. We were less sure of ourselves, as if what we were doing was skirting the line of acceptability. As if being in the car with someone you have known for years, as long as they were of the opposite gender, was an infringement on your standing in the ecosystem of our spirituality and our church.

This is just one example of the types of rules and standards that can and have been put in place not out of adherence to Scripture, but to eliminate any possibility of anything "bad" ever happening. Sure, in many cases, those regulations will, in fact, successfully keep mistakes from coming to fruition. But the damage and counteractive measures have far longer-lasting adverse effects on the individual and the larger church community.

Let's be clear; boundaries can be a very healthy thing. But there is a big difference between boundaries put in place out of conviction or scriptural adherence and those put in place out of fear. Just like Chumra's effect on Jewish students, as exemplified by how many churches have approached directing believers' lives, especially younger believers, it can end up being a detriment to their faith.

* * *

It's a pretty understandable direction that we travel down when we are not assured of God's grace and forgiveness. Suppose you do not believe for a one hundred percent fact that no sin committed can cause God to pull away from you. In that case, it makes sense that you would begin implementing rules and boundaries into your life and the lives of those around you to inhibit you from doing anything wrong.

When exposed to Christianity's ideologies and learning about God, one of the first things brought to the attention of earnest seekers is the reality of their sin and what it does to their relationship with God. This makes perfect sense, as the realization of one's sin, coupled with the revelation of what has been done for us in accordance, forms the backbone of our faith.

We are told that, in essence, our sin separates us from God. This is true, though something that is not always made abundantly clear is that it is not because *He* separates Himself from *us*, or His desire to know or love us decreases, but simply because when our minds and hearts are distracted and feeding into things that are inherently not of God, we lose focus on Him. We are the ones who distance ourselves from God, not vice versa. God never stops speaking to us, leading us, and teaching us, but when we give our time and focus to sin, we lose sight of those things and end up missing out on many of them.

Think of it like this. If God were a human standing right next to you, the ideal relationship with Him would be one in which you are both facing each other, with barely any space between you. When He speaks, you can hear Him, loud and clear. When He whispers, you can read His lips. He can simply make gestures, and you can easily determine what He is communicating to you.

When we sin, two things change, both having to do with us, not God. First, we take a step backward, away from Him, so we are now just that much farther from Him. Second, we turn around, facing the other direction, our back now to Him.

What remains the same? Well, anything having to do

with God. He is still right where He was when we turned away. He is still facing us. He is still talking, whispering, and gesturing. However, things are much harder to decipher and understand from our new perspective. When He speaks, only the things He says clearly and loudly we will hear. When He whispers, not only will we not hear Him, but we also can't read His lips to interpret what He is saying. And forget about mere hand movements and gestures. All of those things will fly right over our head. We will miss them entirely.

Every time we sin, no matter what it is we actually do, we are, for those moments in time, missing out on experiencing God. We are choosing to give our time, energy, and attention to something not of God and thus cannot accept the offerings in which God desires us to participate. No matter what our sin is, what we miss out on in exchange is always the same: closeness and intimacy with God.

God does not change. Ever. He says this quite clearly in Malachi 3:6 when He states, "For I the Lord do not change." I mean... there ain't much deciphering needed for that one. And thank goodness for that. We as humans go through change constantly. What we liked last week we may detest the next. Who we were five years ago may make us nauseous now, or perhaps jealous. On a daily basis, we waver up and down like a rollercoaster.

We are a dependent variable to our circumstances. Everything that happens to us directly impacts how we respond and thus whom we become. But God is not like that. He... is. And no matter what happens, He still is, because everything that happens is because of Him. He is the only true independent variable in the universe. And because of this, we can be confident that He is the only being capable of providing the grace we require to deal with our sin.

* * *

I read something a few years ago about the dynamic between God and sin that has stuck with me ever since and has, in many ways, become a fundamental pillar for how I see the way in which I handle my sin. It's a single, short truth.

God does not react.

Think about it. God is the creator of the universe, overseer of everything in it and everything that happens. He created us, and though He has given us the free will to do whatever we choose, He knows everything we will do and has known since the beginning of eternity.

We, on the other hand, are not like this, clearly. We do not wake up every morning knowing everything that will happen and everything we will do. We may have plans, but never actually know the moment-to-moment details of how they will play out. Furthermore, we do not wake up with a schedule of when we will sin (I mean, some people might, and I would strongly advise you to stay away from those people).

For most of us, sin is a decision made in the heat of the moment. And as such, we usually only have time to come to terms with our actions after the fact. We lie when we find ourselves in a tight situation and need an out, then feel guilty for intentionally giving someone false information. We give in to lust when we decide to listen to our inner temptation rather than have self-control and feel dirty and out of place after.

We react to our own sin almost the same as someone else's, in that we only see it in its true unruly form after it has been committed. It is enticing only up to the point that it happens, at which point it becomes detestable. Our response to sin is most often the guilt and weight of having done something that does not align with the person we think ourselves to be, or at least the person we are striving to become, and the person whom we believe God is calling us to be.

God, however, is an entirely different kind of being. He cannot be surprised or caught off guard. Never once has God witnessed us sin and thought to Himself, "Oh, wow. I didn't think they were actually going to do that. That's a new low. I'm not sure how to respond." God doesn't react to anything because He is the variable to which everything else reacts. He only acts. The problem comes when we place our humanistic response to sin on God, believing He handles it in the same ways we do.

Let's be clear about this. Jesus did not die for the person He "expects" you to be, or at least what we think He expects us to be. He died for the person He knows you are, knowing that that freedom is what will ultimately allow you to be transformed.

Jesus is the only person that will ever know you one hundred percent. He knows every good, bad, and ugly thing about you. Every single part of you. And that's who He died for.

There is no possible way to fake yourself to someone who knows you completely. Unlike every single other relationship in your life, with Jesus, there are no fronts. There are no false pretenses. There are no misjudgments. I know so many people who have been taught to believe that their actions can result in God being disappointed in them, which is just not true. We cannot fake anything about ourselves to God. He sees right through it all, and He loves us infinitely.

Untruth: *God Can't Handle Your Sin*
Truth: *God Doesn't React*

When put into that perspective, I am suddenly relieved of a hefty amount of pressure to meet some type of expectation for God. So many people live their lives, and so many religious cultures are centered around an ideology that they have to perform better and be better if they commit themselves to God. When you decide to follow God and center your life around Jesus, it's as if you now have to be someone better than the person you were before if you want to be worthy of God. This is one hundred percent false and has been the death of the spirits of so many desperate hearts. We cannot impress a God who knows everything about us by trying to be someone we are not.

Further still, we cannot expect to find what will "fix" our broken parts in ourselves. If a car breaks down due to an engine problem, you can't pull over, throw a prayer over it, and wait patiently until it finds it in itself to fix whatever is wrong with it. If the engine is busted, it will not be fixed until you take it in and have someone take a look at it who not only knows the workings of that car inside and out, but also has extensive knowledge of what is needed to fix the problem, along with the steps necessary to do so.

The same goes for us. When we decide to dedicate ourselves to God, our minds and hearts are opened to the riches of His love, grace, and freedom, along with the fruit of those blessings. But we cannot suddenly expect ourselves and others to now magically be able to change the parts of us that may not be entirely right.

If anything, the realization that God is the answer to every ailment of our lives is also the realization that we are not. We are no more capable of fixing ourselves the day after choosing to dedicate ourselves to Jesus than the day before. The difference is that we are now aware of our direct access to the One who can.

My friends and I, who grew up in church together, often share stories of the process of studying the Bible before being baptized. Looking back, there are moments that we laugh at the absurdity of the way some of these teachings would go. We could each recall a particular point in these studies, you know, the *real* studies after we had successfully graduated from our character studies when the leader studying with us would ask us this question: "If you were to die today, would you go to Heaven?"

The point of this question was for us to say "no" and convince us of our need to "get right with God" and be baptized. Only, once we answered the question, the study would be over, and we'd schedule a time to meet next week for the next lesson.

Seems a little counterintuitive, doesn't it? Telling some-one, a kid no less, that they would go to Hell if they died right that very second, and then telling them that they can't get baptized yet because they aren't ready. Yikes.

This was a part of almost every Bible study in our church. There is more than one issue with that, but I want to focus on the belief that we are not forgiven until we have done all the preliminary steps to repent of our old ways of living and dedicate ourselves to God. The phrase "get right with God" is already problematic because of how incapable we are of doing that, let alone the fact that it is somehow now a task we must do to secure our salvation.

Simply put, it doesn't make sense. That idea suggests that our redemption is contingent on our own ability. If this were the case, not a single person would be able to achieve it. We *have* been made right with God. That is what Jesus' sacrifice did for us. It tore the veil. It demolished the brick wall separating us from our Creator. And our faith in what was done for us, as well as *who* did it for us, is what allows us to take part in it.

One of the most significant differentiating elements between Christianity and most other religions worldwide is that nearly every other religion revolves around the concept of personal betterment to earn one's salvation and acceptance. It must be achieved through one's own will and ability. But in Christianity, the truth is that we must accept that we *can't* become better on our own, but there is someone who can, and who even desires to make us better should we let Him. This is one of the biggest proofs that Christianity is the real deal, because we all know deep down that we do not have it in ourselves to truly change in ways that alter the outcome of our lives in any meaningful way. Yet somehow, we continually fall into the trap of still believing that we do.

We are often terrified of our sin, not so much because of what it does to our actual relationship with God, but because we fear how God and others will react. What doesn't help is when we are told in church or by religious peers and leaders that our sin can effectively wipe away God's grace.

Of course, in my experience, it is rarely said so matter of factly. Usually, the result of one's sin is measured up to a big question mark, as if you won't quite know what will happen until it does, so you better make sure it doesn't happen. I have found myself in far too many situations with peers and church leaders where I have heard or been told something directly along the lines of "Bro, be careful. If you keep that up....who knows what God will do?" Suddenly, everyone is a "bro" when it comes to sin.

I never quite knew how to take this. Was it a threat? Perhaps vaguely. Was it proof of some deep conviction of God's damnation on a person for their sin? They may say so, but what it really boils down to is this. They don't know the answer to that question themselves. They have no idea what God will do. They think the fact that they don't know is in itself the answer, but they couldn't be more wrong. There is no mystery to what God will do to sinners who have given their lives to Him and accepted Jesus's intercession on their behalf. And it's not through some torturous punishment. It's just the opposite.

Romans 2:4 says, "Or do you presume on the riches of his kindness and forbearance and patience, not knowing that God's kindness is meant to lead you to repentance?" God's desire is not to scare us into repentance through the threat of damnation and annihilation if we don't turn from our sinful ways. When has that type of enforcement ever worked? His kindness is what convicts us because we know what we deserve, yet God shows us a different way.

The result of our sin doesn't have to be a feared mystery. There is a certainty about what happens when we sin, and it has nothing to do with anything being revoked or retracted. God's grace, love, and forgiveness do not change, as He does not change. God does not react, and has already known of your sin since the beginning of time. It was part of the package deal when Jesus died on the cross. The one definitive answer to what happens when we sin is that it is washed away.

* * *

Have you ever tried building a sandcastle in a river? Not near it or next to it. Standing right in the center.

Does that sound like a futile task? You're not wrong. Imagine being up to your waist in the rushing water, bending over and reaching blindly to your feet, trying to grab that first handful of dirt from the river floor. You manage to get some in your hand, but before you even get a chance to move the dirt into position, the current has already rushed between your fingers and flushed it all away. You pull your hand from the water and see that not a single grain remains. The water took it all.

We are all standing in God's river, being pushed and pulled by the current. And no matter how often we present God with a handful of dirt, it is wiped from our grasp before we ever have the chance to even attempt to make it into a castle. Our sin can't remain with us once we have accepted that the river has the power to wipe it away.

If I had been told this in such a blatant manner five years ago, because of the religious environment I was in, I would have had a nagging thought in the back of my head, insisting that there must be more to it. A catch. What if I sin over and over again? What if the thing I do was intentional, after clearly weighing the pros and cons of choosing God or not beforehand? What if what I did was really, really bad? So bad that nobody knows about it except for me. Surely, then, the implications are different?

Nope.

There was a period during the first few years after I was baptized where I assumed that every time I sinned, I would somehow instantly switch sides from being an ally of God to an enemy. As if God sat on His throne in heaven, His hand hovering idly over a giant switch, half red and half green. Whenever I did something out of alignment with His decrees, He would simply click the red side, and I would be ripped from His good graces. As if now that I had intentionally gone against what I now knew was the truth, God put me on His blacklist, at least until I prayed and repented in an earnest enough fashion to will myself back onto the good side. Then God would roll His eyes exasperatedly, flick the switch green again, and my name would be put back in the book of life. But only until I sinned again. Then it would happen all over again.

I actually had these thoughts. I remember very clearly. Because that's what was taught to me at church. But it wasn't true. Not even close.

God is big. Don't forget it. He is bigger than any idea you may have of Him, and no matter how many times you may readjust that mental image in your head, He will always be so much bigger. This is good news. Fantastic news. Because the bigger God is, the bigger we can allow our sin to be.

Don't read that last part wrong. I don't mean that because of God's magnitude we can sin more often and in bigger ways. What I'm saying is, however big you believe God is has a direct correlation with how honest you can be about your sin.

If you believe that God is small, unloving, unforgiving, or maybe doesn't have the power or ability to forgive all your sin, you will not, *cannot* admit to the severity of what you have done, because if it is made known that what you did was as bad as it actually is, and God *can't* do anything about it, then you're stuck. But, if your God is big, as big as He wants you to know that He is, and capable of dealing with anything you throw at Him as if it was child's play, you can accept how short you have fallen because His power is enough to overcome it.

There is nothing we can do that is beyond the power and protection that Jesus' death provides us. No matter how hard we try or how far we walk away from God, His promises never weaken, and His love never fades. His grace is not denied from us or lessened in any way. Our salvation is secured no matter what we do.

Untruth: *We Can "Out-Sin" God's Grace*
Truth: *God Has "Out-Graced" All of Our Sin*

This truth, this promise, is the greatest, most powerful declaration in the Bible and is meant to be the framework of our entire faith. Oftentimes the word of God is called "the Good News." This is why. This *is* that news. But somehow, so many churches and believers have fallen off the trail and lost sight of it. Instead, we have substituted this relatively simple idea for a complex framework of half-truths, intertwined with false beliefs and misinformed notions, which only lead to two things: fear, and out of that fear, rules.

7

A FAILURE TO COMMUNICATE

Rigid. That's the word I would use to describe the dynamic between guys and girls in my church growing up.

When you're young, it's not as easy to identify any rift between the people around you, as everyone is friends with everyone. But around middle school is the time when it began to become apparent. Everyone is told to take a seat during a Friday night devotional, and there ends up being a near perfect split of guys on one side and girls on the other. This was the norm, and how it almost always was. Despite the obvious desire to co-exist and interact with the opposite gender, the fear and pressure of the eyes on you for doing so outweighed it.

In every social situation, my guy friends and I would be in groups consciously separate from the girls. Yes, we did talk with one another, but there was almost always a palpable tension, as if you were under a spotlight, and every word you said or glance you gave would be scrutinized extensively. This made for awkward interactions, rushed conversation, and an overall inability to simply be around anyone of the opposite gender. It was just easier not to be.

From my own experience, there was usually an agitation with the girls in our age group, as if any interaction with them more than a simple greeting and a goodbye would result in more trouble than any of us had any time or mental capacity for.

Why was this? Why was there this practically unanimous sense of tension and estrangement among the young people in my church? Was it any of our faults? I believe one of the most significant factors catering to this mentality and life-style was that, in our minds, interacting with the opposite gender was the easiest way to end up doing something wrong. This wasn't something we came up with ourselves. It's what we were taught in our youth ministry.

From our earliest years, it was common to have lessons and discussions about the dynamics between guys and girls. Yet, practically every time, it felt that the amount of time spent divulging all of the negatives and risks far outweighed the positives and great things those relationships had to offer. We were young, innocent, and, most of all, trying our best to do the right things. Which, sadly, took the form of self-improvement and seeking to stay on the good sides of church leaders rather than beginning to seek and learn about God's grace and freedom.

In many ways, the opposite gender was the closest you could get to staring temptation directly in the face. For us guys, girls weren't the devil. Of course not. Because that was a silly thing to say. Yet, the way we lived and viewed them in reference to our standing with God nearly fell in line with the belief that the most potent obstacles to our faith came directly from our involvement with them. And the things we were being taught in church did little to negate those suppositions.

The time between elementary, middle, and high school was one big contradiction. On the one hand, we knew that those of the opposite gender weren't bad in and of themselves. We were all experiencing that desire to be close to them. We all had crushes, and as we got older, those crushes developed into deeper longings. We were never told that anything about that was bad. But it was made definitively clear that, should we attempt to develop an actual relationship with a girl beyond simple friendship, we would need to be absolutely sure that we had our priorities in check and our heads on straight.

Even when the opportunity came, and we found ourselves confident in where we were in our faith and as people, there would be someone, somewhere, who would sow seeds of doubt into our minds that would move the door we were about to open ten more steps away. We would be tossed into a pit of fear, insecurity, self-doubt, and an overall sense of distrust in ourselves to carry a healthy relationship with someone of the opposite gender. We were taught not only not to trust the priorities and agendas of the opposite sex but also that, even if we believed we could trust ourselves, we could never be sure.

Tell that to people in their thirties, or forties, or fifties, and you would still leave them thinking it over for who knows how long. But begin sowing those ideas into children, indoctrinating them into the train of self-distrust over the course of years while they are still figuring out who they are as people, and you will leave a slew of unhealthy ideas and mentalities that ingrain themselves so deeply into who they are that it can take years to unlearn them, if they ever actually do.

That is what my peers and I, as well as countless other young people in churches all over, have been and are currently experiencing. Until you get older and see the damage it is doing to yourself and those around you, it is a near impossible dynamic to get out of because it is directly intertwined with your faith. Not only were we cautious about the opposite gender because it could lead to "bad things," but those bad things could very possibly destroy our entire relationship with God. And we wanted God. Even though many of us were still trying to figure out who God was and where He fit in our lives, one thing we knew was that we didn't want to jeopardize the possibilities over something as trivial as a girl.

But there was still that desire. Interacting with the opposite gender is a learned skill. It may sound silly or perhaps like I'm overcomplicating things, but it's true. The way guys interact with girls, and vice versa, requires a different approach than talking with your regular friends. Having friends of the opposite gender is just as crucial to your growth and development than a person in your core group of friends of the same gender. There are different things to learn and skills to hone. That's how God designed it. And in an ecosystem where that wasn't encouraged, it made for an environment that was clearly desperate for it.

One of the most prominent signs of this was that every interaction between a guy and a girl seemed to come with an expectation that something meaningful had to happen. By "meaningful," I mean anything worthwhile that is more than formality. Something soul feeding. Did we know that at our age? Absolutely not. But I know that for me, I felt the weight of making an impression during the fleeting moments of every interactions I had.

If you haven't experienced this, it will probably sound like I am reading too far into it. But for those who have, you know that reading too much into every single occurrence was precisely how it was for us going through it. Every interaction with someone of the opposite gender was riddled with mixed signals and sloppy communication. And not even for people who had an interest in each other.

Much more commonly, platonic aspirations were just as subjugated to this same effect.

Most people just wanted to be friends and be around the fresh air that came with those interactions. And for those who did have deeper intentions, everything was that much worse. I know this from experience. In a church situation like the one I grew up in, "liking" somebody was the first step to being completely socially isolated from them. With everything from indirect notions from leaders to directly being told to stay away from each other, it was a playground of mental torment.

I write all this wishing I had known these things back when I was going through them. But how could I have? To many of my peers and me, it was normal. Even when it didn't *feel* right in our hearts, like something was off, we didn't have any other perspective to compare it to. So, when circumstances arose where it was clear that something was wrong, the blame often fell on things other than the wrongful standards of our church.

* * *

When I was twelve years old, I developed a crush on a girl in my church. In a normal world, it would be expected that our interactions would be awkward because of how young and inexperienced we were in these types of social interactions. But for us, not only was it completely awkward, it was slightly chaotic, because both of us had completely underdeveloped muscles for how to engage each other, even compared to the standard for kids our age.

On one particular Sunday, several friends in our church group were hanging out at the house of one of our lead pastors, and before we could sit and think it through, a game of Truth or Dare had broken out. I know, I know. A group of co-ed middle schoolers playing truth or dare. What could go wrong? Within ten minutes, I was dared to kiss this girl on the cheek, and after a few minutes of reluctance, I gave in. And then it was over. Or so I thought.

Not so many days later, I was in my room reading a book when my phone started to blow up with calls and texts. It was a Friday night, and at that moment, there was a youth ministry devotional taking place that I hadn't been able to attend. Unsurprisingly, people had found out what had happened, and as a result, the ministry went into what felt like a complete spiritual lockdown. The text messages and voicemails were borderline chaotic, as peers and friends told me what was happening at the devo. Apparently some hurtful things were said to some of the people involved, which resulted in hurt feelings and a large display of emotion, leaving everyone trying to piece together what had happened.

Within the coming weeks, conversations were had with all the kids involved, in groups and individually. At the time, it had felt appropriate enough, as we knew that there were better things we could have been doing than playing Truth or Dare. I had also assumed that the parents were being filled in by our youth leaders regarding what was happening, but it wasn't until years later that I found out none of them had been told anything. My parents knew about the Truth or Dare game because I had told them myself, but that was the only information they had ever received about it. If they had known then that the youth ministry was reprimanding us, they wouldn't have been happy, as what began as procedural attempts at resolution quickly turned into something far greater. For one, it didn't stop. After the talks were had and the feelings were mended, the matter didn't seem to be dropped.

This whole incident happened in the summer, right

before our church's annual Youth Camp. Though one of the points of camp is to escape from our day-to-day lives, that year, it felt like the drama of the situation back home followed me up the mountain. During our five-day stay, even more talks were had with all of us.

I remember one in particular, after the night's final camp-wide devotional, where those involved in the Truth or Dare game sat in a circle of plastic fold-out chairs in the middle of the meeting hall with two of our ministry leaders. By that point, I was beginning to feel far more than a kid's usual remorse for playing a game of Truth or Dare. Though it was a summer night and hardly very cold, I couldn't stop shivering for the entire meeting. I wasn't even cold. My body simply wouldn't stop shaking.

Yet, this meeting (where, mind you, the same things were discussed and mulled over) still didn't mark the end. It felt as if these talks were no longer about trying to resolve any untended feelings but rather attempts to drill into us the gravity of the situation to dissuade us from ever doing something of the like ever again. Which, trust me, we were already inclined not to do after the first talk we had.

The next day, our entire ministry was asked to meet in the bleachers of the outdoor soccer field. Everybody was there. Not just me. Not just those few who were a part of the Truth or Dare game. Everyone. For what felt like hours, I, as well as the others involved, had to sit among all of our friends and peers, some who knew about what had happened and many who had no clue, while our leaders once again discussed what had happened.

Looking back, I remember feeling like a criminal, as if I had committed perhaps one of the darkest, most damaging crimes that would potentially have forever-lasting consequences.

Everyone in our youth group was now aware that something had happened, and it sent an almost immediate ripple through our entire group, which lasted for what felt like years. The already palpable rigidity had escalated, and there seemed to be a new element in the fold: a deep-seated mistrust of one another. Not necessarily to any one person, but just as a whole, guys against girls and girls against guys. Something big had happened, but whose fault was it truly? The guys or the girls? Sides had been taken because, in a way, sides had been created by the dynamic of how things were being handled. This situation was simply the catalyst that forced them to be actualized.

It felt to me that most every person had zero trust in any member of the opposite gender, and as such, a faction-like dynamic began to develop. Back then, having no idea of anything unhealthy happening except my own failed attempts at liking a girl, I thought it was my fault. That somehow, the entire change of atmosphere in my group of friends was the result of what I had done wrong.

That stuck with me for a long time. It was something that I took on that, in many ways, latched onto me as a sort of label, something I now felt guilt and shame for, yet wasn't my fault at all. It was the natural progression of a seed already planted years before, and as we all grew older, it began manifesting in more direct ways.

* I wanted to add something here, as this past week one of my closest childhood friends came to visit and we got talking about all of our experiences growing up, and in this specific instance, all that unfolded as the result of that game of Truth or Dare. According to him, the effects were not just felt by me, which wasn't surprising. One shocking discovery was that, until very recently, my friend had been under the impression that something much worse had transpired between this girl and me, and he was

amazed to learn that it was just a quick kiss on the cheek. During the talks with our whole ministry, it was never divulged precisely what had happened, only that something bad had gone down with several kids. It hadn't occurred to me until this recent conversation that many people never actually knew the details of what had happened, and only had the contextual clues to try to put the pieces together themselves. Based on the extremity of how the youth leaders handled everything, my friend had just assumed that what had happened was a much bigger deal. With their minds left to wander, you can probably imagine what they came up with. For years, this experience weighed on me, and even to this day has left a much bigger impression on me than it should have. After all these years, I have been able to delve into it and figure out exactly what I believe about it. But at twelve years old, being subjugated to those very same ideas made me feel like I had the weight of the world on my shoulders, and I carried a deeply seated shame for many years. What's worse is that I believed my parents were being told everything that was happening, and because of that, I assumed they condoned the actions being taken, which only further validated my feelings of shame. But they were never told, nor were any other parents, about what was happening.

My peers and I went through a very clear transition when we went to high school. All of these same dynamics were still present, although in many ways began taking a backseat as we all grew older and naturally became more confident in ourselves. Girls and guys spent more time together, though much of the tension was still there. The playing field had changed slightly, but the faulty foundation was the same.

It was a very interesting time because, on the one

hand, guys and girls hung out much more regularly. That "faction" mentality had begun to dissolve, and we felt more unified. But the misdirection was only getting worse, only in less conspicuous ways. That mistrust, which for a time had been palpable, was now more closeted, though still very much present. At this time, we were being taught things in the teen ministry about one another, both verbally and through our experiences, that only made us more untrusting not just of the opposite gender, but also of ourselves in how we interacted with them.

Things were said along the lines of, "That person doesn't have your best interests at heart" or "That person will hurt your walk with God." To be sure, these types of things can be helpful to know if true, but the problem arises when someone dictates to you what they think about somebody else, when in reality it is very likely not true whatsoever.

The reasoning for all of this was the sole goal of making sure none of us made any mistakes. "Mistakes" is a pretty vague term, in this sense relating to anything from surpassing physical boundaries to gossiping or other typical teenage drama. Anything that fell out of line of the path we were set on in our relationship with God, which, for the majority of the time, was defined not by us, and not even by God, but by our church leaders.

I get it. None of those things are healthy; they really aren't, which is why the intentions behind these norms are understandable. But a significant aspect of the equation left out of this scenario is having the faith that what you are sowing into us as young people will result in us developing our own convictions and standards, rather than forcing us to keep away from things so the opportunity to do something wrong never presents itself. Ultimately, that won't result in people with deeper moral convictions. It will only result in people who have never had the chance to develop those convictions by themselves.

For years I grew up not having the faintest idea that anything was wrong about the ways in which we were being brought up. I never questioned it. And a big reason for that was that the things I was being taught at home were unquestionably sound and stable. Both of my parents were devoted Christ followers, and raised me in an incredibly healthy way. Neither of them would ever agree with many of the things my friends and I were being taught as we were growing up in church, and the times when they heard about such things, they were some of the first to vocalize their concerns.

The problem was how little they were actually made aware of, and how out of the loop they were kept from the inner workings of our church's youth ministry. In many cases, it was an intentional lack of communication by those in charge. Though, at the end of the day, nearly every youth leader only wanted the best for the kids under their care, there was an unhealthy precedent set towards the "trust" the parents needed to have in them when it came to the ways they were leading their kids.

And even though they believed the ways they were leading us were in our best interest, there is no doubt in my mind that the lack of communication with our parents was partly due to a knowledge that not all of their ways of doing things were right. The scales were so tilted that, should a parent express even the slightest bit of disagreement to the ways in which things were being handled in the youth ministry, their own commitment and trust in the leaders and church in general was put into question.

My home life was very nurturing and healthy when it came to leading me toward God and filling me with accurate beliefs about God and how I should live my life. So, as a result, I also saw the ways I was being raised in church as just as healthy. I assumed everything that was being taught to me in the youth ministry was condoned by my parents, so it never crossed my mind that any of the ways I was being raised could be damaging or toxic.

I know many others who shared this dynamic, wherein their home life accurately reflected and upheld authentic Christ-centered convictions, but because of the disunion and lack of communication between parents and youth leaders, the lines between what was good and what wasn't were blurred inordinately.

* * *

When you get baptized, you suddenly find yourself in a whole new landscape of living and thinking. The stakes are raised, as now that you have decided to devote yourself to God, the expectations placed on you heighten to meet the standards of your declaration. Many of these higher standards are good and healthy because they are in step with how God desires us to live. But like we've established, this is also the time when you are exposed to the less than beneficial practices that come less from God and more from the Church and its own agendas and ideologies.

When I was first baptized in the ninth grade, I was eager and excited to be called to these "higher standards" of living my life in accordance with Jesus. We all know the things God wants for us often take sacrifice and intentionality and usually aren't the easiest, at least from a material point of view.

I wasn't alone in my intense desire to live as closely to how God calls us to live as possible. Many of my peers were in the same boat. That commitment, that ambition is, at its root, not a bad thing (if only we could keep hold of that authentic tenacity throughout our lives!). The problem was, while we were filled to the brim with fervor, we lacked any real experience, and thus nearly every aspect of how that eagerness was put into action was dictated by what was told to us by older Christians, often church leaders.

This is not partial to a church environment. It is the same for nearly any area of life. Those without experience learn the dos and don'ts from those who have already learned them. In the same way, the entire direction of how you live and think about the world can be the result of just the few people closest in proximity to you during the years when you are most easily influenced.

This can be a great thing if those older, more experienced people you find yourself around really have their heads on straight. On the flip side, however, if the people of authority and influence don't hold the healthiest beliefs, perspectives, or practices, there is no way of knowing until you have found yourself adopting the same.

This is one part of life we have very little control over, since during the time of our lives when we act as sponges, absorbing as much as we can from the world and people around us, we don't yet have the knowledge or awareness to know if what we are taking in is actually what is best for us. Only when we are older are we able to see the distinction. That's why so many people spend years, decades, even their entire lives trying to undo and unlearn many of the effects of the thought processes they have since realized are not healthy or what they believe.

If a church is founded on partially-realized truths, then its people will only be able to live partially-realized lives and have partially-realized relationships with God. So many people are stuck in this scenario without even knowing it because, as far as they have learned from those around them, they have the whole picture when in reality, they are missing large portions of it.

As young Christians, this is the exact situation the majority of my peers and I found ourselves in. We were sold on the Bible's promises, but then subjected to lifestyles grounded in only parts of them. The remaining percentage of these promises, the unknown, were instead filled in with fear.

I wanted God, just as most of my friends did. We knew that much. What we didn't know was how much of what we were being told about what God wanted was accurate and what was actually keeping us from recognizing God's true nature. It wasn't until around tenth grade that I began to be presented with situations which slowly started to show me the cracks in these fear-based ideologies.

And, of course, it all started with a girl.

8

ABOUT A GIRL

It always starts with a girl, doesn't it?

Looking back, with the understanding that I have now, there are so many points where I think to myself, "Man, how did I not see it THEN?" But that's the danger in it all. You don't know what you don't know.

In tenth grade, I left my traditional high school to be homeschooled with several other peers from my church. And of course, like any mediocre teen B-movie, there was a girl in that group that I had… taken a liking to. Mind you, she was the only girl our age in the entire class, which led to a whole different arena of conflicts, as you can probably guess.

Well, we started talking, then talking more, and then even more. It was clear from pretty early on that we both had feelings for each other. At this point, I had little experience with a mutual interest in the church, and every step was uncharted territory for me. Once it was apparent that there was something between us, I was intent on doing everything I could to make it work in a respectful and spiritual way.

Looking back, I think those aspirations were even greater due to what I viewed as a pretty poor track record. Up to that point, the only other situation I had been in with a girl I liked who liked me back ended in what I deemed a disaster, leaving lasting effects on myself and my friends that I believed might never be forgotten. As you can imagine, I was determined not to let that happen again.

At the time, we were around 16, and the idea of dating wasn't necessarily a destined next step. For me, "making it work" simply meant accomplishing three things. First, to get to know her better and develop a friendship. Second, to do it in a way that honored God. And third, if things ended up not working out, to be able to say we both learned and grew from the experience, and nothing ended on bad terms. To say the bar was low would be an understatement.

From almost the very beginning, we were both extremely open with our parents, and they were all very encouraging about it. I remember a conversation with my parents where they asked what I thought the next steps should be to get to know her better. I wanted to do it God's way, and we all thought it would be helpful to get the insight of one of the head pastors of our church, who was also one of the head leaders in the youth ministry. Within a few days of reaching out to him, he picked me up and took me to lunch.

I was nervous, but excited, knowing this physical step meant that it was real. There was a girl I liked, and I was taking steps toward actually doing something proactive about it. I had a goal, and I was achieving it. I was being a man, and a man of God at that.

I don't remember much about the conversation we had. I'm sure there were a bunch of formative questions about her and me, how long we'd been talking, what I wanted, etc. I do remember the outcome, however. And I was excited about it. *"This is a great thing, and you should want to honor God through it all,"* which I did. *"You should both want to make sure nothing gets in the way of your relationship with God."* Of course. Check. *"So, considering you've been communicating quite a lot, you should stop texting for the next two weeks"...*

I should've known then. But then again, how could I have? It made sense, at least in the way he presented it. Nothing is more important than my relationship with God, and we *were* texting a lot, so giving it a break for fourteen days cold turkey would be a great opportunity to hunker down and sort ourselves out spiritually before... before what, exactly? We weren't planning on jumping in and dating. We just wanted to get to know each other better. Of course, I didn't take that train of thought at that time. I was on board. Willing to do whatever it took to ensure it was done "right." And here was one of the leaders of my church telling me what "right" was. Who was I to question it or think otherwise?

Around this time, I remember more than one instance where different friends of mine were made aware of how open I was being with my parents and church leaders about liking this girl. They were a little older than me, a few grades above me in school, and had pretty strong reactions to my transparency, warning me not to be open about it with any more youth leaders. According to them, the more people we told, the more at risk we were of being separated, put in different Bible groups, and being restricted from talking or texting.

I thought their adverse reactions were uncalled for and inaccurate. Sure, people have bad experiences with stuff like this. But to resort to *not* being open about it seemed like the wrong conclusion, and I disagreed with them. I was new to the high school ministry, and I was determined to do everything in my power to lead a healthy relationship with a girl I liked. Little did I know that these older friends had learned the lay of the land and knew what we were dealing with before I did. It was only a matter of time before I learned as well.

Two weeks came and went.

We didn't text. It was a bit of a downer, considering we were talking a lot and growing closer until we just... weren't anymore. But I felt that by telling her it was part of a "plan," I was leading her, and God was being glorified. Near the end of those two weeks, I was scheduled to meet with another teen leader to figure out where to go from there. When we talked, I expected the outcome would be that the girl and I could talk again, with some new guidelines for going forward, the "next step." But instead, he told me that we should continue not to talk. I don't remember the reasoning. But I remember feeling disappointed. I was ready to go forward, but it didn't seem like anyone else was prepared for us to do so.

We continued our streak of silence. Two more weeks. Then another. Then some more. It ended up staying like this for *months*. Whenever I had a conversation with someone of authority, I hoped it would clarify what to do next. But it never happened. There was always another reason why we should continue to distance ourselves from each other.

After a while, I started to see that there was a problem, but not the one I now know it was. In one particular instance, my dad contacted the head youth leader questioning how things were being handled. Rather than explain to him why they were going about it the way they were, the leader simply said, "I'm his leader, don't you trust me?", to which my dad replied, "Well, I'm his father. Don't you trust *me*?"

I was often reminded that this girl and I were "the

guinea pigs," and everyone, including the leaders, was learning how to go about it as we went. Fair enough. One thing I had begun to take on, as more and more of my peers started to find out about me and this girl, was the desire to show people that it could be done. A guy and a girl could successfully have a thriving relationship in our church, and it was worth the work. For up to that point, the success rate was extremely low, and the number of dating relationships of anyone in the church under the age of eighteen was... well... none. I wanted to show people it was worth doing it God's way. This was my chance to help mend the tear between the genders in our youth group that I believed I had caused.

As time went on, we both began to grow impatient. Can you blame us? The time came when we both didn't quite know why we still weren't "allowed" to talk, and it seemed no one else did either. We both had been keeping an open dialogue with our parents, who, though they were support-ive, seemed just as unsure as we did. I knew my parents disagreed with the directives I had been given. Yet, even so, there was a boundary to what extent that differing of opinion would actually matter. The church leaders didn't want us in contact for some reason. Was it me? Was it her? Thinking back to the doubts I had about myself during that time, I can only imagine what she must have been thinking about herself as well.

Eventually, it became unbearable. We were entirely in the dark, being fed tidbits here and there that seemed more of an attempt to subdue us rather than to help guide us to where we wanted to go.

At one point, we started commenting on each other's social media posts. Then commenting on each other's comments. Soon, we were having full-on conversations in the comment sections of Instagram and Facebook posts. After all, they said we couldn't text. This was public, and anyone could see our conversations. It wasn't sneaky or deceptive in any way. Neither of us felt like it was anything worthy of trying to hide. We just wanted to connect.

How sad is it that this was the result of the situation we found ourselves in? Before being open and honest about liking each other, we talked every day, and were really getting to know each other. We never crossed any lines or did anything that would be considered wrong or unhealthy. Yet, as soon as we decided to let people in in the hope that they could help us develop an even deeper, stronger relationship, we were cut off from each other completely. Quarantined from each other. And now, several months later, our only form of communication was through the comment sections of social media posts. Even then, we felt like we were skirting a line, yet if asked, neither of us would have any clue what that line was.

* * *

While we couldn't text, we did see each other in person multiple times a week. Not only did we have church get-togethers every Sunday and Friday, but we also had many homeschool classes together throughout the week. But due to the feeling of such scrutiny from the people around us, there was such an overwhelming amount of pressure when we actually saw each other in person that most of the time, we wouldn't even talk.

By this point, it felt that everyone around us knew about our situation. It was rarely discussed openly, but it was often the topic of conversation in smaller, closed circles. And it was weird. Really weird. In homeschool, there were only a handful of people in the entire class. And at church, our friends were all part of the same social circles.

It certainly didn't help that the head of our homeschool group was the head pastor's wife, who had all of the knowledge of our current situation. Additionally, several of the other parents were also leaders in the church. All eyes were on us, all the time. We never got a break. Even at school, there wasn't a time when we weren't under the surveillance of people directly connected to our situation and had some kind of authority or say over it. And every leader knew.

I remember an instance when we were both invited to the birthday party of a mutual friend, and, though for the majority of the time we kept in very opposite directions of one another, there was a fleeting moment where, as we were all walking down the street in a large group, our strides synchronized and we were able to chat. Within seconds, another friend of ours came up from behind, wedged himself between us, and pushed his arms out in either direction, separating us as he yelled "Distance!" over and over again, loud enough for the entire group of friends to hear.

It was meant as a joke, as we *were* friends, and though I knew he had no ill intentions, the girl and I were both simply at the point where something like that was enough to shut us down completely. We felt like prison inmates, under constant surveillance, and when we stepped a single foot out of line, we were reprimanded publicly and beat back into submission. The mere fact that our painful situation was such everyday discourse that a complete outsider to it knew enough to make such a joke was a testament to how convoluted it had all become.

There was even a point where all of the youth ministry leaders had gone on a retreat, and it was revealed later that one of the main topics of discussion was this girl and me.

I'm sorry, what? We liked each other. That's it! Yet it was being treated like we had gone up on stage one Sunday, snatched the mic from the preacher, and announced to everyone that, at sixteen, we had decided we were getting married and were moving to Antarctica.

Everything we did seemed to result in some sort of critique, or worse, further impediments. All we wanted was to develop a deeper relationship, yet it seemed like that desire was an impossibility, and became less and less likely with every effort made.

We both wanted to talk so bad every time we saw each other, but we just couldn't do it. We were both completely psyched out of our minds, on the brink of paranoia. Actually, I wouldn't even say "brink," as in many cases, I blatantly recall anxiously glancing around and playing through every possible scenario in my head whenever it even crossed my mind to go and talk to her. There were times when one of us would get the courage to make the intentional approach and start a conversation, but even those moments were full of nervous glances and quick, awkward exchanges that would be cut short as soon as someone else would approach, or even if we thought there was a chance someone *might* approach.

In the rare occurrences where we really needed to talk about something, we had to intentionally plan out when and where (via the Instagram comment section), which was usually someplace far away from other people. You'd think I was meeting up with her to sell her drugs, yet we just wanted to hear each other's voice. But one thing's for sure. We definitely felt like criminals.

It was torture. I so clearly recall the amount of time collectively spent "preparing" to see her on a given day before church or school, going through what talking points to bring up, but in the most condensed, direct form possible because I knew our time would be fleeting. Having to rely so heavily on social cues, given by her and others around us. Being so uncertain about how she felt towards me and how I wanted to make sure she knew I felt about her, without *real, normal* communication. And on top of it all, having the weight of knowing that so many others were looking to us to see if we would be able to pull through to the other side.

In a very real way, how our situation ended up playing out would dictate how many of the young people in our church would decide to go about liking someone in the future. Everyone had a stake in it, whether they knew it or not. If it worked out, then there would be proof that being open about who you liked paid off. But if not, it would be further evidence that it was simply a lost cause. I felt that weight every day. Yet I was already being crushed by the weight of everything else.

Every time we would leave an in-person event, we would contact each other almost immediately after in the comments of an Instagram post to get a feel for how the other person felt about the attempts made at contact that day and if they even still had an interest. Imagine someone telling you that they liked you and then being unable to talk to you for months. To leave you on that kind of cliffhanger, without a chance to process or solidify those feelings, would leave you a complete wreck. Especially if you liked them as well, and suddenly there was something very real on the line.

That's when we started using the ping pong ball. Every year at Youth Camp, one of the most popular activities during free time was playing ping pong. During the week, my friends and I would spend hours huddled around the table, trying to defend our titles. That summer, I had somehow come home from camp in possession of one of the balls, and, immediately, a game began to develop between the girl and me, where whoever was in possession of the ball would try to pass it off to the other without them knowing. We would sneak it into bags while talking, put it in pieces of schoolwork, anything we could think of.

We kept at it for what must have been months. Each time we came into possession of it, we wrote our name somewhere on its surface before passing it back. In a very real way, this lame, angsty game became a sort of saving grace for us, as it provided us an intentional reason to approach the other person, despite our deep-rooted inner fear and anxiety of ridicule. If we missed the opportunity, the game wouldn't progress. So we had to utilize every church or school gathering.

By the time that ping pong ball was eventually taken out of commission, it was dirty, dented in several places, and covered with so many of our crisscrossing signatures in all kinds of inks and colors that you could hardly see the white surface beneath. That ping pong ball brought some much needed levity to the otherwise chaotic and confusing circumstances. Once it was gone, everything continued the way it had been going.

Every year, our church held an annual "Family Camp" where families went camping for a weekend (a complex concept to grasp, I know). That year, we were both really excited at the possibility of having the freedom to talk without the feeling that everyone was watching us. We were away on a mountain in the woods, for crying out loud! If there was any chance for us to be out from under the spotlight, it would be there.

For once, there wouldn't be a thousand eyes on us, and we would be able to be normal. We weren't even planning on hanging out the whole time. No. Prior to that weekend, we had preplanned a specific time when we would meet at the bleachers of the basketball court to have a ten-minute talk in person (Mind you, I know the term "meeting at the bleachers" often carries another meaning to many teenagers. But we were homeschooled Christian kids! Being able to sit next to each other and talk was the furthest either of our minds went).

The day came, we met at the bleachers, and for about four minutes we got to actually enjoy each other's company. But then, a voice called my name from what seemed a long ways away. Way down near the other side of the camp was the father of one of the families, who was also a youth leader, calling me over to him. I left the girl waiting in the bleachers and went to talk to him. He only asked me one question. "You think that's a good idea?"

He didn't tell me what I was doing right or wrong. He didn't give me any sort of definitive statement at all. All he did was leave me further questioning my decisions. Besides, his face told me that, no matter what I thought was the appropriate answer to his question, he had already come to his own conclusion. From my perspective, it just seemed like he wanted me to know I was treading on thin ice.

I don't remember what I said in response. But I remember not going back to the bleachers to finish that conversation.

I think, overall, one of the hardest parts about it all was not simply the fact that for such a long time it was impossible for this girl and I to talk to each other, but that during that entire time, I had to struggle with the fact that she was able to speak to every other guy in our ministry any time she wanted. She had a good number of close guy friends, and I had to watch them get closer and closer to each other while we could barely make eye contact in the same room. All because we were open and honest about our feelings for each other. And trust me, what I said about wanting to show people it could be done right? Well, what everyone saw gave them the exact opposite notion. The message they were all undoubtedly left with was that if they ever had any hope of being able to have a relationship with someone they had feelings for, they should *never tell anyone*. Especially in the church. After a while, I started to feel the same way.

* * *

This went on for well over a year. Of course, a lot happened during that time. Talks with leaders and peers, talks between leaders without either of us even being there, etc., that kept us feeling like we were still heading towards *something*. But nothing ever happened. We were both close to our parents, and kept them in the loop throughout everything going on. After we finally began to see that it was a hopeless cause, we decided that perhaps the church's advice didn't always need to be the final say. After talking with both my parents and hers, it was agreed that we all thought it would be a great idea for me to ask her on a date.

Now, I think it's important to note what I mean by "date." Growing up, you didn't go on traditional dates, as in one-on-one outings. In high school, you went on "encouragement dates," which were always in groups and were designed to eliminate as much interpersonal focus as possible. Yet even though these events were barely reminiscent of a date, each person did have a specified date who they were paired with. After discussing the possibility with both my parents and hers of asking this girl on one of these encouragement dates, we all believed it would be a fantastic opportunity for us to just be able to hang out together.

And so I did. We went on a date with a few other of our friends from our ministry. And it was the first time since admitting that we had feelings for each other that we felt we could be ourselves around each other and simply *exist* around the other person. It was a much needed breath of fresh air.

That is, until our church leaders found out. Specifically, one leader had gotten word that we had gone on a date against the advice they had given us. And they were not happy about it. The next thing I knew, the people around me, from other leaders and teens to random church members, had heard that we had "crossed boundaries." In one scenario, two close friends of mine were advised by their mother not to hang out with me anymore because she had heard that I had crossed boundaries with this girl.

When you hear that phrase, I'm sure many things come to mind, most of them a lot worse than deciding to go on a group date together after we had decided *with our parents* that it was okay for us to do. Yet people started coming to me telling me they had heard we had crossed boundaries, and seemed to believe we had committed some cardinal sin. Little did they know what we actually did to warrant such a title.

Once word of this got to my parents, they decided to call this youth leader to straighten things out. They wanted to ask why this leader had come to such a conclusion and provide them with the correct details of what had actually happened.

When they got on the phone and asked this leader if they had been telling people that we had crossed boundaries, the leader explained that they did and "had good reason." My parents asked for further explanation, and the leader went on to say how they had explicitly told us not to go on a date, and we did it anyway. In their words, "He completely disrespected me!"

Now, they were right about one thing. We hadn't done what they had advised us to do. But, we didn't simply decide to rebel and do something that we knew was wrong. We expressed our viewpoints to our parents and made a joint decision about how to go forward. This teen leader was hardly the only person I sought advice from during all this. As a matter of fact, it would have benefited me greatly if I had asked for *fewer* people's advice, as in my determination to give myself the best foundation for success, I had reached out to quite a few people for guidance. Because each person had a slightly different stance on the matter, in the end, no matter what I chose to do, it was contrary to multiple people's advice.

Yet that is precisely what advice is, or at least what it should be. It is guidance freely offered, with no forced contractual agreement that the recipient must adhere to it. This leader had somehow been convinced that their say in the matter, though simply advice, was, in fact, the unarguable final say, and doing anything contrary to that advice was to be disobedient. They believed they were the ultimate authority in my life, which simply wasn't true. It was looked at as disobedient when I asked this girl on a date against her advice, though funnily enough, all of the people I sought advice from gave me a thumbs up to do so, *except this one leader.* So, if we wanted to split hairs, I was *following* much more advice than I was refusing.

It was a broken system, an extremely unhealthy environment, where no one person had the same stance as another about what to do. The problem at the end of the day was that they believed that something had to be done to prevent the possibility of a future bad decision from happening, rather than encourage and set us up for success in keeping God first in our relationship, which we were both already inclined to do. They cared about us, which I knew. But in some twisted way, in order to keep us safe, they put us in a place where we always felt like we were standing on the edge of a cliff.

* * *

This all continued on for a few years, through the remainder of high school. At some point, we started texting again. I don't remember if there was an official "go ahead" from a leader, but a point came where our parents, who were intent on playing active roles in the situation, finally agreed that enough was enough. They trusted us, which in the end, should trump any decision by a church leader.

However, throughout the entirety of the following three or so years, people on both her side and mine were still actively and consistently giving us erroneous advice and information that ultimately ripped away any remaining confidence we had in ourselves to try to attempt moving forward. There were times I clearly remember seeing the girl sitting alone with a church leader across the church courtyard and *knowing* they were talking about me. I never knew what they were saying, but I had already begun to develop such a distrust that I believed whatever was being said was most likely directed against me. And in the times when I did find out what was being said, I often wasn't proven wrong.

This wasn't a one or two-time thing. It happened constantly. She and I were continually pulled aside by leaders and friends, or called on the phone and asked to talk about problems they seemed to have with our relationship, which all this time was still simply a friendship. What really struck me the wrong way was that we were never once talked with *together*. It was always separately. And it was almost always because they wanted to maintain complete control of *our* narrative.

In the end, the misdirection and confusion induced by those three influential years resulted in so much baggage and uncertain feelings that the cost no longer felt worth it, and our friendship fell apart because we never got the chance to set the foundations for a healthy and growing relationship. Third parties began getting involved, and some real problems began emerging between the two of us. And then, *then,* for the first time since this whole thing started, we were asked to sit down to talk with a leader *together.* Because now it wasn't about leading us towards a fruitful relationship. It was about being able to help pick up the pieces and prove to us that they were right all along. At least, that's how I felt.

Learning to deal with your feelings is one of the most daunting and confusing landscapes a young person must navigate. When you're a teenager, learning your way around dealing with an interest in someone is already such a complex and intimidating space to be in, without any religious interference. When having to deal with not only the uncertainty of mutual feelings for someone, but also how to go about it through their church's obstacle course, many people simply don't have the mental or emotional capacity to deal with it.

Doing something God's way may be more difficult sometimes, but in the end, is always abundantly fruitful. However, when we let fear dictate the processes through which we conduct ourselves, we add a level of complexity that is simply not needed. The result is never fruitful, but usually full of hurt, pain, and often a perversion to God's will. I personally know of so many people who, due to similar experiences in environments such as the one I grew up in, no longer want anything to do with God. Because for them, what they have been taught has led them to believe that what they experienced *is* God, when in reality, it was anything but.

I didn't even touch on how this dynamic evolves for people in their twenties and beyond. I've known countless people in the church who have had interests and, in some instances, were dating in their twenties and even thirties. From their stories, the number of hoops they had to jump through, and were still dealing with, was insane.

In many scenarios, it was as if the relationship did not consist of two people, but three, the third being their church or a specific leader or authority positioned between them. The end result was that nothing the two did was ever alone, or even entirely independent. It was always influenced or vetted by this third party. These people are treated as if they should not and cannot be trusted with anything on their own, and as a result, they, in turn, start thinking the same about themselves.

> **Untruth:** *You Can Never Fully Trust Yourself*
> **Truth:** *You Can Fully Trust God to Guide You*

This dynamic extends far beyond the confines of guy-girl relationships. The modern church is full of people who have been taught that they can't trust themselves, and because of this, a codependence has emerged in almost every aspect of Christian culture. Everything people do, say, and think has to be overseen and allowed by their church before any decision can be made or action can be taken. I do not believe this is a coincidence, but rather a deliberate attempt at acquiring and holding as much control as possible over believers and their individual lives. Healthy churches don't do this. Period.

The biggest problem with this is the fact that so few people seem to have a problem with it. Many people can't seem to imagine it any other way, simply because they have been told that this is God's way, and any desire for things to be done differently is to be prideful, rebellious, and in the end negligent of God. Which leads us into the next rung of this ladder.

PART III

REPERCUSSIONS OF RIGID RELIGIOSITY

9

WHAT IS SPIRITUAL ABUSE?

So far, I've illustrated in depth the first few years of my high school experience in my church. As I mentioned, there was a point where I finally began realizing that there were problems in the way things were being done, or rather, incrementally, I began to see these issues more and more clearly. As it goes, it seems the more aware you are of the things that are wrong, the clearer you begin to see the way everything truly works. My particular instance of liking a girl helped me see an undercurrent that flowed through my entire church in many different areas.

By seeing how my church operated, I soon understood that many other churches, and areas of Christianity as a whole, have developed and operate similarly. What I would quickly realize as I began witnessing the less than flattering ideologies in my church is an idea that I had never before been exposed to... Spiritual Abuse. Interestingly enough, though I had never dealt with the term until that point, I, as well as the majority of the people around me, had been experiencing it for years without even knowing it.

What is spiritual abuse? You grow up hearing about

many types of abuse: physical, verbal, sexual, mental, emotional, psychological, domestic, even animal abuse. But spiritual abuse rarely seems to be a hot topic in ordinary conversation. According to Lisa Oakley and Justin Humphrey, authors of the book *Escaping the Maze of Spiritual Abuse: Creating Healthy Christian Cultures*, spiritual abuse is defined as "a form of emotional and psychological abuse that is characterized by a systematic pattern of coercive and controlling behavior in a religious context." Some of the forms this type of abuse may take include:

- Manipulation and Exploitation
- Enforced Accountability
- Censorship of Decision Making
- Requirements for Secrecy and Silence
- Coercion to Conform [inability to ask questions]
- Control Through the Use of Sacred Texts or Teaching
- Requirement of Obedience to the Abuser
- The Suggestion That the Abuser Has A 'Divine' Position
- Isolation As a Means of Punishment
- Superiority and Elitism

I realize that's a lot to process in bullet point form. But I hope the concept is clear. Spiritual abuse is, by this definition, exerting power or control over someone using the ideas of religion, faith, or beliefs. We see extreme examples of this often in movies or television shows, in which church congregations are being deceived into mass cult-like groupthink, often by one sole pastor or leader, usually for the result of money or to carry out some other dubious goal. And while it is sometimes exaggerated in entertainment and media, much of it is spot on and, unfortunately, happens a lot.

Now, my own experiences aren't as extreme as some of the ones you may hear about on Twitter and see in Netflix documentaries. But think about this. If, in these severe cases, the people in these churches were usually oblivious to any manipulation or abuse, how much harder is it to spot the less conspicuous forms spiritual abuse can take, especially to those experiencing it from the inside?

If you are brought up being told that the way things are being done is the way God wants them to be done, the barrier preventing you from understanding that it is, in fact, wrong is that much more difficult to perceive. The truth is, though the presence of spiritual abuse in many religious communities is much more understated than the extreme examples we often see in media and entertainment, the effect it has had and continues to have on so many people cannot be taken lightly.

Over the last few years alone, there has been a rising tidal wave of voices from those who have been neglected and abused in places where they trusted they were safest, places where they are supposed to be protected. God is a protector, a shield, a refuge. He is a voice for the voiceless and a healer for the wounded, but He is being misused as a device in which to help gain control and power over others. Thus, instead of being the face of love and grace, He is being made a scapegoat for the wounding and pain being dealt to the people most earnestly seeking Him.

Spiritual abuse warps our perception of God because it paints an inaccurate picture of who God really is. When it feels like His love, forgiveness, and mercy are not strong enough motivators to push people in the direction they want them to go, churches and their leaders will resort to presenting a stricter, harsher, and less loving God in an attempt to scare and smother people into submission to their agendas. In many cases, the god that ends up being preached resembles so little of who God actually is, embodying so few characteristics of the authentic God we crave to uncover and know. A cheap, dollar store copy is chosen over the priceless original because the church's goals became more important to its leaders than God's will.

The thing about this "pseudo-God" that is erected is that he is also a weaker God. If God is big enough, powerful enough, and loving enough to handle all of our problems, heal all of our wounds, and forgive all of our transgressions, then there is no force strong enough to cause people to act. At least, this is the lie that churches who preach this pseudo-God fall for. They pick up the idea that if there is no fear of what may happen to us if we don't follow God's decrees, no point at which we could potentially find ourselves denied of God's blessings, love, and forgiveness, then we won't be driven to listen and follow the church, specifically those in charge.

In many scenarios, the idea that a relationship with God is an uphill climb is appealing to misled church leaders because it promotes the necessity of a white-knuckled, gritted teeth approach to religion, where only those with the most fervor and drive make it to the top, and one miscalculated step can send you tumbling all the way back down to the bottom of the hill. These leaders, who seek power and control more than anything else, desire followers who will put the mission of the church above all else, and one of the easiest ways to accumulate them is by convincing them that advancing their church's specific agendas is the fastest, safest, and most assured way up that hill to God.

If you desire to control someone, convince them they have a problem that only you have the answer to. A relationship with God is not a problem. It is a solution, *the* solution to every problem that arises in our day to day lives. God is our safe haven. He is our peace amid war, our drink in the middle of the desert. He is the relief to every ailment, yet too many people's experience of Him is somewhat the opposite. Although they may be convinced deep down that this is still the case, what many people are actually experiencing when it comes to God and their spiritual life is less freedom and peace, and instead an overabundance of emptiness and longing.

Spiritually abusive leaders and churches take the blessings and promises of God, which He offers to us freely, and put them behind paywalls of service and dedication. Yet, it seems that no matter how dedicated or "fruitful" one is in their walk with God or service to their church, the true essence of those blessings is always one step out of reach.

So many Christians never experience the true nature of God, not because it doesn't exist, or because they weren't good enough to experience it, but because their church has sold them on a lesser God, who is naturally more inclined to send you to Hell for your shortcomings than to begrudgingly be convinced that you have done enough good to change His mind. Many people believe that God is good and loves them for who they are, yet have been trained to approach their relationship with Him like a tightrope walker, where the path to salvation is a near impossible feat, while the opportunity for failure and damnation is imminent and nearly inescapable for the ordinary, unperturbed believer.

The majority of these people will live their entire lives without ever realizing they were being fed a lie. But even sadder still are the ones who *do* see that the way they have been living was a detriment to their wellbeing, but wrongly place the blame on God, not realizing that He was as much a victim of the situation as they were, and the root of the problem was the false image of Him they were being presented.

We all know people who have "tried Christianity" and are now averse to anything having to do with God or the Bible. Maybe this person was you. Perhaps this person is *still* you. Things are thought and said to the likes of "If this is God, why would I want anything to do with Him?" The answer is simple. You wouldn't. You *shouldn't*. And those who put that together, especially those who have experienced the effects of spiritual abuse, want nothing to do with church or God again.

We live in a generation of hurt people; unfortunately, a large percentage of that hurt can be attributed to spiritual abuse. People are living their lives believing that God is someone they would never wish to cross paths with, as in many cases they have, and what they were left with was less than satisfactory. If only they knew that God, the *true* God, is just as aggrieved by their hurt and pain as they are, and wishes they only knew what He could offer them if they knew Him for who He truly is.

* * *

From what I have already described of my own experiences thus far, several items listed as characteristics of spiritual abuse can be observed. Growing up, I had very little idea that anything was wrong, but now, it is more evident than ever just what I was dealing with. And once I understood something was off at church, it seemed that the signs of spiritual abuse began to become more and more obvious.

One of the first direct confrontations I remember having with this concept was not long after I had begun talking with my parents about what I was witnessing. I kid you not; within a matter of days, I received a text from one of the youth leaders asking me why I was talking to my parents about any of this stuff at all. It was a question, yet simultaneously pulled the silent weight of a threat. As if what I was doing was wrong, and by sharing with my parents what I was going through, I was infringing on ground that I did not have permission to tread. Growing up, I told my parents about everything and, up until that point, had never been questioned for it. It was then that I realized that the spiritual environment I had grown up in, which I always believed to have my best interests at heart, was harboring loyalties to other people and things that weren't God.

Now, I want it to be said that the role that church leaders, especially youth leaders, play in the lives of kids and teens can be unquestionably invaluable. I owe many of my past leaders for so much of what I know and believe about God. But there is a line that needs to be defined between what place they have when it comes to authority over the people they lead. At the end of the day, *all* authority over a child falls to their parents. No matter how present or involved, or how seemingly capable or not, parents always retain complete control and authority over their children (at least, until they are eighteen and can make those choices for themselves.)

By challenging my decision to talk with my parents about my experiences in my ministry, this leader conveyed the assumption that final authority over me and my choices fell to them, even over my parents. And whether or not they would admit this if asked, expressing their desire that I withhold information from my parents (aka requiring my secrecy and silence) was an act that clearly demonstrated their disposition.

Some parents want to be much more involved than others, and some are more physically and emotionally available. Where the need arises, those who take it upon themselves to be an active part of a young person's life are truly honorable. Yet there have been situations that I have witnessed and been a part of where authority is almost "seized" by church leaders upon assuming the need. For someone to offer help when they feel called is one thing. But authority is not something that can be taken. It *must* be granted. And even then, everything done and advised under that authority is *still* under the parents' jurisdiction.

There are far too many churches and spiritual communities that I have known personally, and unfortunately far more that I don't, that have normalized the relinquishing of authority over younger members to the leaders of their youth groups and young people ministries. As such, so many things are done and taught that are not only not condoned by the parents, but aren't even made known to the parents at all.

This mentality cannot remain. Despite all of the reasons someone may argue why young church members could benefit from church leaders having some amount of authority or final say in their lives and decisions, it is not healthy, and is not biblical. In a situation like mine, where my parents were undoubtedly the ones where final authority fell, a leader wanting things to be kept from them is the epitome of unhealthy boundaries and a completely wrongful exertion of authority.

Church leaders and any older, wiser person can have such an invaluable and fruitful influence on a young person's life. I'm sure we can all call to mind those individuals in our own lives who took the time to sow into us wisdom and knowledge, offering the best parts of themselves to us simply so that we can become better people. Don't be mistaken. There were many such people in my own life and church whom I will forever be grateful for. Dynamics of this nature set a perfect precedent for how these relationships should work. Guidance can be offered. Advice can be shared. But whether or not those offerings are accepted cannot be tied in any way to an individual's perceived obedience, church stature, reputation, or relationship with God.

As I began to see the darker realities of what was going on in my church, my first response was not to believe it. I didn't want the things I saw happening to be true, as this was where I had grown up, and had for nearly the first two decades of my life viewed as the absolute healthiest and most God-centered place I could ever be. I gave the benefit of the doubt in any situation I could to anyone whose actions and intentions I felt may have been misjudged. But as these hopeful graces proved to be routinely given in vain, I began to be forced to see the present circumstances for how they really were.

Which led me to my second response, which was to look at other churches and spiritual communities dealing with spiritually abusive systems, and compare my circumstances to theirs. By comparing the severity of these other churches, and other denominations for that matter, I could see my own church's problems as much less serious and the problems I was facing as nit-picky at their worst.

But I knew that wasn't true. I saw how the people around me were being affected, and knew how I was personally dealing with the detrimental effects of the harmful environment we were in. It may be true that some people had it worse in other places. But does the fact that someone else is going through a more challenging experience invalidate the reality of your own?

This realization brought me to my third response to the true nature of what my church was and had become.

I was sad.

10

A SYSTEM OF SHAME

Shame. I'm sure we are all familiar with this term to some degree or another. It's an idea preached as what we are freed from in Christ, yet it is a device constantly used to debilitate and minimize people, especially in a spiritual environment.

Shame is the currency of a spiritually abusive ecosystem. It is the fuel without which abuses of control and power would not be maintainable. These types of high demand/high control environments could not exist without shame, as shame is the primary method by which the members of a church are debilitated, invalidated, and convinced that they are valueless as individuals. Thus, anyone who truly desires a relationship with God must rely on those of authority to successfully prepare and lead them to Him.

Most of our biggest, deepest wounds come from shame, regardless of whether or not they were inflicted in a spiritual environment. It's the voice in our head telling us that we are not enough, and never will be. That we are broken, and always will be. It is the crippling inner stigma we hold of ourselves that makes us believe we are chronically and inescapably lesser-than.

Now, there is a clear distinction between shame and guilt. While guilt is a feeling toward your actions, shame is a feeling toward yourself. We've all felt guilt for things we've done. We are born with the inclination to feel guilt when we do something wrong. It's how God designed us, to feel in our hearts when we do something against whom He calls us to be.

Shame is in many ways the opposite, as instead of contrasting what we are with what we've done, it tells us that the things we've done are in direct correlation with who we are. I'm sure we all have personal experience battling the effects of shame encroaching on our self-image and self-worth. When you do something wrong, especially if you find yourself continually doing it, you begin to feel that maybe it *is* who you are. Even when you grow and change, sometimes you can't seem to leave that thing you did in your past, well, in the past.

It doesn't help when it seems like those around you who should be helping you see that you are not your past are instead making you feel the most condemned. I've learned that guilt is rarely ever "placed" on you by someone else. Usually, that feeling comes from within. Shame, however, seems to primarily be the effect of external influence. The only reason we feel lesser-than is because we are either told that by someone around us, or the way they act or respond brings us to that conclusion ourselves.

I say this because if shame is an accumulated result of our interactions with others, the people around us have a very hefty influence on what we think of ourselves. No matter how unhealthy it is, a good amount of our self-image depends on how others treat and talk about us. If they tell us that something we did was wrong and, therefore, we are inferior, that idea often plants itself in our minds and, over time, evolves into a much more deeply seated idea.

Growing up, I always heard stories of the earlier days of my church. Interestingly enough, it was often to show how much worse things were back then compared to how they were now. A common narrative had to do with the ministry's hyper-fixation on evangelization. This is an extremely common attribute of many churches, regardless of denomination. After all, Jesus tells us to bring people to Him, and churches want more people, so the connection seems like a no-brainer. But in this case, the role that evangelizing played was anything but natural.

When my parents were in their thirties, much of their standing in their church was tied to the effort and success of their evangelization. Bringing guests was a necessity at nearly every service, small group, or other gathering. The number of people you reached out to was kept track of. Leaders literally had notes tallying the number of people you were able to bring to church every month.

The reasoning for such extreme measures was genuine enough. For the majority of leaders and members, growing the church was perhaps the most pertinent and beneficial act of service and obedience to God. The act of sharing our faith with others and leading more people to Christ was seen as direct proof that one's faith was deep and mature. If you managed to bring in a bunch of new faces, you were considered a respectable and highly spiritual member of the ministry. However, if for whatever reason your attempts weren't as fruitful, well...

You were put on the list.

More specifically, your name was added to the "Weak

and Concerned" list, aka the list of every member the church leaders deemed weaker in their faith and needed to be put under stricter management.

Now, I believe it's important to note that, as it goes for many of the things discussed in this book, the original intentions behind such a list were not hostile or malicious. At its conception, the purpose of the Weak and Concerned list was to denote those in the church in need of support. Whether experiencing financial or marriage troubles, or struggling with their faith in general, those in need of prayer or other forms of support were added to the Weak and Concerned list so that the other members of the congregation would be made aware of the need, and have the opportunity to step in and offer their assistance in whatever form they deemed necessary. The *intention* behind the list was good. Unfortunately, the environment in which the list was implemented already catered foundationally to a skewed perception of what it looked like to be spiritually mature or spiritually weak. A precedent had been set for the defining characteristics that signified those who were struggling in their relationships with God, and more often than not, these characteristics correlated with how effective one was proving to be in their evangelization efforts.

As a result, the list quickly began taking the form of a correctional leaderboard rather than a tool to help people, being filled less by the names of people who actually needed support or prayer, and more by those who were considered to be "underperforming" in the areas the church gave as indicators of the strength of their faith.

One-on-one talks would be had between leaders and those on the list about how they were concerned for that person's spiritual stability. Awareness would be spread to all leaders, and often other church members, that that individual shouldn't be put in any ministry roles that included spiritual responsibilities, as they weren't mature enough in their faith to handle such positions. But the lasting effect of such a hierarchy was the shame it induced.

While your name was on that list, it was accepted by those around you that you were indeed weaker in your faith and, as such, were at risk of pulling others down around you. When everyone else around you was trying their hardest to do the Lord's work, your faith in God wasn't deep enough or mature enough to prompt you to do the same. And because of that, God was disappointed in you, and so were those in your church.

For many people, this dynamic resulted in quite the opposite effect of the list's original intended purpose. Instead of being encouraged to admit their faults and needs in order to seek support, church members were eager to do whatever they could so as to *not* have their name added to the list. And because the dominant factors in deciding whether or not someone was to be added were based heavily on outward performance, many members resorted to approaching their church life, and thus many facets of their faith, as a checklist of things they needed to do and results they needed to achieve, even if their hearts weren't in it. They showed up. They said the right things. They put on their biggest smile and gave one hundred and ten percent in what the church required of them.

And, of course, they evangelized.

They set the fire of God in their heart and made it a personal creed that not a single person would cross their path without being made witness to the incredible impact Christ has made on their life. Oh, and make sure they agree to be their plus one to that week's Sunday service. And also hopefully convince them to come to the midweek the following Tuesday. And maybe, just maybe, if they tried reeeaaaallly hard and really let God speak through them, they could even get them to agree to have a conversation with the head pastor. Then they'll be in for sure. Completely sold on the message and mission of the church and ready to become a fisher of men themselves.

At the end of the day, these church members weren't reaching out and sharing God with people because they cared about that person and their salvation. At least, not entirely. Sure, that could have very well been a part of it, and it often was. These people loved God and wanted others to know Him too.

But when that alone was not a strong enough motivator, the thing that pushed them to get people to agree to come to church was the fear of the shame that would inevitably be bestowed upon them if they showed up empty-handed. It was the disapproving looks from across the room. It was their small group's indirect yet simultaneously judgmental inquiries regarding their efforts to reach out that week. And ultimately, it was the silent assumptions of themselves and those around them that it must be the result of a deficient faith.

In these scenarios, being able to bring someone to Christ was an absolute win, but a lot of the time, it was more of an added bonus than the primary goal. People evangelized because they loved God. But the act itself was often done out of a fear of what would happen if they didn't.

* * *

My mom recalls a specific moment from her early days as a Christian that exemplified the stringent measures taken to ensure church members were evangelizing.

"Women's Day" was an annual event held by their church, and every year, the biggest focus during the weeks leading up to it was on reaching out to and getting as many confirmed guests as possible. Back in the day, the church owned and met at a club in Hollywood. Yep, that's right. Several times a week, the congregation would meet smack dab in the middle of Hollywood for church gatherings.

On this particular evening, the women were meeting together for their midweek service. The "Women's Day" event was a week away, and before a single Bible was opened, they got to the most important matter of the night: who was bringing visitors.

The Women's Ministry leader stood at the front of the room, the eyes of countless anxious women watching her nervously, for they knew what was coming.

"If you have ten or more *confirmed* visitors for Women's Day, raise your hand."

A handful of arms lifted into the air, accompanied by enthusiastic applause from the rest of the occupants in the room. The hands lowered.

"If you have *nine* confirmed visitors, raise your hand."

Again, several hands were raised, followed by a similar, yet slightly less avid round of applause.

The countdown continued.

"If you have *eight* confirmed visitors…"

"If you have *seven* confirmed visitors…"

Hands were raised, followed by an applause of slowly decreasing enthusiasm, until finally…

"If you have *two or less* confirmed visitors for Women's Day, raise your hand."

Slowly, tentatively, a smattering of hands lifted into the air, this time followed by no applause, only the sympathetic glances of those around them.

"Keep your hands up…"

The ministry leader's finger bounced around in the air as she counted how many hands were raised. Once she had a tally, she continued. "We're going to start the lesson now.

Those with your hands up, we're gonna go downstairs for a meeting. We will see what your obstacles are and how we can help you get visitors confirmed before next week."

All those who hadn't managed to confirm an acceptable amount of guests did as they were told and were led downstairs, where they would be met with another ministry leader who would guide them through a discussion about why they had failed in their Christ-commanded responsibility to invite visitors. It wasn't uncommon in these meetings for people to be told that they were letting God down by failing to reach out to people for God's Kingdom, and that those dealing with shyness were actually in sin.

Luckily, my mom had managed to acquire a satisfactory number of visitors for the gathering, and was able to stay in service. Unfortunately, her friend sitting next to her wasn't so lucky. Later that week, the friend talked with my mom about how bad she felt, not because of how she was being treated, but because of her own perceived shortcomings for not being able to secure visitors. As she explained to my mom, she was not a native English speaker, and the language barrier was a huge obstacle when attempting to reach out to people. She was also highly introverted, and was told that night that being introverted was a sin she was failing to overcome.

This woman was not an anomaly. So many just like her have completely bought into the idea that their value and importance to God and the church comes from their performance and success in arbitrary measures of spiritual devotion erected by people who seek numbers and influence over leading people to God. Because they don't know any better, they believe it when they are told the most prominent sign of their spiritual health is their ability to provide for the church.

They feel great when they are successfully able to do so

because their church, leaders, and peers treat them with sincere respect and spiritual regard. They make them feel valuable. But when these people find themselves unable to meet the standard set for them, they question every part of themselves in relation to their standing with God because those around them seem to be telling them that they should be.

The way that so many churches view and deal with evangelization is just one of an extremely long list of ideas and practices that may be taken from the Bible in some form, but remodeled to serve a completely different agenda. God's word and these humanistic standards of Christian living are seen as one and the same, rather than the two wholly different principles that they are. And when we find ourselves being accused of not adhering to these practices, or simply underachieving in them, shame is often used as a tool to motivate us to reevaluate our priorities. And the most unfortunate thing about it is, in the short term, it works.

Untruth: *Every Church Standard is God-Willed*
Truth: *Some Standards are Simply Church-Willed*

When it comes to the implementation of shame-based motivators to serve a biblical principle, there may be no better, or more harmful, example than purity culture. I know that many, if not all, Christians are familiar with the concept and tenets of such a system. The intensity of such a culture differs significantly between churches and denominations, and for a long time, I viewed my church as being on the lighter side of that spectrum. And though, while I still believe there are spiritual environments in which the effects of purity culture seem much more excessive than the one I grew up in, I have come to realize that, in many cases, the ramifications are just better disguised.

I'm sure for some of you, just the word "purity" causes your heartbeat to quicken and your palms to get sweaty. Trust me, I understand. Growing up in church, the word was used so often that it didn't register until I was in college how uncommon the term is actually used in everyday conversation. It's like referring to your phone as a "cellular device." "Let me just grab my cellular device real quick." "Have you seen my cellular device?" "Do you have any games on your cellular device?" See what I mean? It's just not a common way to speak. It still makes sense, but in many cases, it's almost *too* correct.

The same goes for "purity." Outside of a religious context, I would think the areas you would hear the word the most would be in reference to water, or perhaps a gem or crystal. Only those with a higher degree of knowledge and understanding in their respective field would use the term in such a practical manner. But when you're a part of a religious community, the word rolls off the tongue as easily, and nearly as often, as talking about sports or the weather. And the reason is understandable.

The Bible has a lot to say about purity, and not defiling ourselves or separating ourselves from God by taking part in impure acts. There are varying types of purity that the Bible talks about, including purity of heart, purity of mind, and purity of body. However, the most prominent aspect of purity that people seem to like focusing on (I wonder why), from which purity culture is directly contrived, has to do with sexuality.

As God created sexuality to serve and glorify Him, we are told that we should not abuse it in ways that pervert the true nature that God desires it to be used. I believe that to be incredibly true and a very healthy attitude and disposition toward our sexuality.

God wants us to have as little standing between Him and us as possible. He knows that when we give ourselves to things that "contaminate" (not just in a sexual way or having to do with the idea of being "dirty," but also in terms of holding to things that aren't of God), there are more obstacles that come in the way of us being able to be as clear of heart and conscience as possible to be able to receive God most intimately. In this respect, not only does the Bible implore us to keep away from such things, but it even tells us that, "... among you there must not be even a hint of sexual immorality, or of any kind of impurity, or of greed, because these are improper for God's holy people." (Ephesians 5:3, NIV)

Suppose we genuinely desire to be as close to God as possible and strive to eliminate as many things that may obstruct or distract us from that intimacy and clarity as possible. In that case, God tells us that there should not even be the tiniest speck of impurity. That would make perfect sense, as the absolute best scenario of eliminating such impure elements would, in fact, be the disassociation from *all* things that fall under that umbrella. It's not merely some lofty goal for Christ-followers to set their eyes on; it's a command from God that is encouragingly attainable for us, not through white-knuckled self-exertion, but through the power that we can share in through the Holy Spirit.

However, by the way some religious environments attempt to maintain this "Not A Hint" mentality, many may wish that it was simply a figurative ideal. In far too many contexts, this idea has been taken to such an extreme that what now stands is a system that completely misrepresents those original intentions and, in turn, has replaced them with a legalistic framework whose sole purpose seems to be to produce shame. Purity culture promotes the elimination of impurity and any and all possible avenues to immodesty through means of harsh and often abusive forms of self-hindrance and intense denunciation.

In a community adherent to purity culture, the sanctity and retainment of one's purity comes above any and every other cause or purpose in the life of a believer. In most cases, though God is claimed as the reason for such measures, He becomes an afterthought to the rigorous and harmful environment of self-correction and the underbelly of mistrust and remorse of oneself and any person who could threaten one's own purity.

As many know, the extremity of purity culture standards is usually very different between men and women. As a man, my own experiences would probably be classified under the mild, more common preemptive church purity measures.

It was a ministry-wide regulation that guys and girls should under no circumstances talk or text after ten o'clock at night because, as we all know, after 9:59, even the most sincere male Christ follower morphs into a hormone-induced sex monster.

At camps, guys and girls had separate designated swim times. When at the pool or beach, we were advised to keep our shirts on so as not to cause any of the girls to "struggle" (Honestly, I'm sure not all of us were good-looking enough to even be a problem, but to only mandate the golden-tanned, six-packed guys might have presented an even bigger issue). There was one particular time I remember a fellow teen getting reprimanded for wearing a tank top to youth group because his bare arms were causing problems with the ladies (One can only dream of being that ripped).

Though these efforts always felt somewhat comical and futile, at their worst, they were simply annoying, though they could also encroach on how we as men viewed the danger we unwittingly posed to women. There were many times when the message being sent was that we were threats, no matter how good our intentions were. Despite this, the impositions of purity culture most heavily fell onto the shoulders of women, and the lasting effects of shame and self-contempt are nearly incomparable.

Women are responsible for men's purity. That is the message that purity culture proclaims, and is the basis for the crippling and dispiriting conventions placed on women in churches that adhere to it. As such, it is their responsibility to live in such a manner that inhibits the possibility of men to "stumble" (another word that we rarely hear outside the context of religious talks of sin and temptation), and it is also their failure should the men around them succumb to worldly temptations.

The history of the church is blanketed with the commonly held notion that men are incapable of being in control of their sexuality. While they may be able to manage certain aspects of their approach to their purity, the insurmountable force of the elements around them, namely women, poses a threat that they simply cannot overcome.

The expression of sexuality is much more visual for most men than it is for most women. This is just a scientific fact, and alone is not a problem. In fact, it is the way God created it. However, this does mean that the external forces around them, primarily the way that women look, dress, and act, has a more significant and immediate effect on them. Again, this is how God created it. Where this equation begins to run off course is how we navigate this distinction.

Instead of training men in Christ's ways of mastering our sexuality, we as a society and church have effectively put most of the responsibility on women. The way they dress, the things they say and do, and even deeper aspects of who they are are micromanaged and vetted by those in spiritual authority. Women are told that their worth as people, sexual partners, and children of God is directly affiliated with their submission to these principles. Thus, when someone is seen as not meeting the standard, their value and self-worth are run into the ground.

* * *

Looking back, I don't think any of us knew how bad it actually was in our church, especially not the guys. If you had asked any of us if we thought there was something wrong with how some people were being treated, I doubt any of us would have denied it. But we had been taught to trust the decision makers, and that trust often trumped our own perception.

Sure, the way some of our peers were being treated at church seemed off, maybe even a little harsh at times. But it was justified. There was a clear way that things were done, and when someone didn't seem to want to adjust, disciplinary action seemed inevitable, sometimes even necessary, for the good of everyone else's faith and spiritual health. Yet most of our opinions were founded on faulty information and grounded in a distorted view of the people around us.

Everybody in our church knew Riley (not her real name, but I was given permission to use it). We had been Sunday school peers since we were children and had grown up together. Through years of church camps and youth groups, we had become well acquainted and, at times, would even consider each other friends. The rest of the time, however... Well, we were pretty much the opposite. Not enemies, per se, but I always kept my guard up whenever we were in the same room.

You see, Riley was known by everyone, and not for the best reasons. She liked to live on the edge, consistently skirting the line between right and wrong and often falling face first into the latter.

Riley had a reputation among her peers, and the church as a whole, for always managing to find the trouble, especially when it came to boys. She was always hanging around them, and in many cases, it seemed wherever she went, drama was never far behind. What exactly was she doing that was getting her into so much trouble? We could only imagine. There were always rumors and gossip that she was doing "this" with that person and doing "that" with this person. For the most part, the conclusions drawn were primarily pulled from the public responses of church leaders.

It felt like at nearly every church gathering, she would end up being sat down by a leader to have a conversation about her questionable actions, or often be asked to leave altogether. She was sent home from camps. And in the rare times when nothing happened, she was always under the surveillance of watchful eyes, ready to pull the trigger should she even attempt to step out of line.

This was no secret to anyone. In natural response, the boys tried to stay clear of her at all costs, not wishing to be the next guy caught up in any emotional turmoil, while the girls kept their distance to avoid being confused as a "troublemaker" like her. In both cases, the intention was the same. Nobody wanted to be associated with Riley because they didn't want to risk their reputation.

As we got older, her treatment by others, especially church and youth leaders, worsened. She was all but removed from the youth ministry entirely, and at the gatherings she was given permission to attend, she was often separated from the rest of the group. She was rarely at the fun stuff like baptisms, parties, or hangouts with friends on the weekends. I remember at our church's unofficial graduation celebration for my senior class, there was a table where every graduating student had a framed picture and a box with their name on it, where friends and family could leave letters of congratulations. Everybody had one, except Riley.

She had grown up in our church and had been there for as long as I could remember. She had even been baptized several months prior. Yet even when the students who had been a part of our ministry for less than a year were included in the event, she was excluded entirely.

She was, however, at the graduation. Seeing her name missing from the table, my mom and I were able to put together a makeshift box for her and add it to the bunch. I don't know if she saw her name missing or not. Regardless, I'm sure it didn't take a missing picture to make her feel like an outsider.

If I hadn't known any better, I would have said it felt like she was being erased from the church's memory. But I did know better. We all did. Because most of us had grown up with her and knew the kind of person she was. Though I felt bad enough to attempt to lessen the blow, I still believed it was for a reason. It had to be. Because that's what we were told.

After we graduated and all our friends split off, some going to college and the rest moving on with their lives, Riley and I lost contact. At least, we lost as much contact as possible in a world constantly connected through social media. It seemed that I wasn't the only one. None of my close friends talked with Riley anymore. Most didn't think anything of it. Some were even relieved.

Recently, Riley had begun sharing posts about spiritual abuse on Instagram. Having been going through a similar stage in my own life, I reached out, and we started talking about all of our "crazy church experiences" growing up. I definitely didn't expect what she was going to share. I thought I knew who Riley was, but it turns out, I barely knew her at all.

Here is just an excerpt of what Riley had to say:

"When I finally left the church after years of abuse, it has taken me years to be okay again. The people were well meaning, but they didn't know what harm they were doing when they were doing it. I was never told that I had any say in my own life. The moment that I showed my stubborn individuality I was singled out, monitored, and counseled what seemed like every minute of every day.

When that didn't do the trick to subdue the thoughts, actions, and rebellion, they isolated me. I was kept from attending camps with my peers. I was put in specifically picked groups away from my friends, and was set aside from them whenever we were together. Eventually they started kicking me out of camps altogether. All I did to get kicked out was hang out with boys too much against advice. Mind you, I had never even kissed a boy. All I did was express a healthy amount of sexuality in those groups of my peers.

As I got older, I never stopped expressing myself and my sexuality, but I started to believe them when they told me it was abnormal and excessive. According to them, liking men and flirting were all sins. I quickly started to hate my sexuality. I was constantly confessing my "sin" of my desire to be in a relationship. I was always being told to suppress the desires. When I became a teenager, my family started going through hardship, and I was isolated from my peers and painted in a negative light to them constantly. My anxiety and depression surfaced when I was about thirteen. I believed that I was a horrible person and was the cause of my family's pain. I believed I was a slut. I still had never kissed a boy.

By this point, I had been kicked out of my peer group at church because I "wasn't a good example" and I was no longer allowed at camps. I wasn't even allowed to sit with my peers in church. I started to spiral, and began to self-harm as a way to distract myself from the pain inside. Nobody knew how to handle me. At school, my grades and behavior plummeted, and my parents were finally made aware of my depression in eighth grade after I was reported to the dean by someone who saw the cuts on my legs. I desperately sought some form of connection, but I was still forcibly isolated from my peers, and had been made out as the "dangerous outcast" by the church.

I had no friends at school either, and was homeschooled in an attempt to handle my depression and self-harm. I wasn't even allowed to leave the house unsupervised. But my depression only got worse the smaller my world became. I was desperate for any validation of who I was, even turning to online chat rooms, which resulted in my internet being taken away. I had no support system of any kind. I was completely alone.

By sixteen, my symptoms had only gotten worse, and I was sent to a psych ward. The night I was being transferred, my parents got a good look at the words that had been scarred into my leg: Slut. Liar. Alone. No One Cares. I had never even kissed a boy, and I had carved the word slut into my leg. I was only sixteen and had been shamed by full grown adults so badly my entire life that I believed I was a slut and was damaged beyond repair.

I never got the chance to really sit with myself and feel how beautiful my soul was, by itself, without having to run every thought, action, and possibility through a million other people's opinions. I got so caught up in what the church wanted me to be and who they were afraid that I was that I lost sight of God, Jesus, and the beautiful person that they loved and created, who was perfect just the way she was."

There are very few things in this world more powerful, and more dangerous, than a false narrative. As God is truth, it is the responsibility of the Church to lead people toward what is true, toward God. Our trust in our churches is that, in listening to their teachings and heeding their judgments, we will be guided toward truth and away from the myriad of false ideas in the world.

But this isn't always the case. As Riley's story illustrates, sometimes the most harmful ideas are not about the world, but ourselves. A single idea has the power to topple an empire, and has on many occasions. What, then, could such an idea do to a soul?

Of nearly every one of my peers, Riley was the most open and expressive of her desire to be with the opposite gender. Looking back, her actions weren't even abnormal or unhealthily excessive. But compared to the rest of us, who, for the most part, had succumbed to the intense austerity and suppression of those desires, she stuck out like a sore thumb. And because of that, she was subjugated to any and all measures of discipline deemed appropriate; aka, her narrative was ripped apart. And not only did everyone around her believe it. She believed it herself.

We had all grown up viewing Riley as an example of what happens to someone who has weak boundaries, doesn't follow the rules, and doesn't listen to authority. According to the narrative we were given, she had done all the wrong things, and we allowed that idea to justify how she was being treated.

Of course, we had no clue just how bad it was. And none of us had any idea how false the narrative was that had been erected around her in an attempt to suffocate her to the point of conforming. But we knew enough. And we did nothing, because we believed it was okay. In the name of righteousness, we allowed Riley to be the butt of the jokes, the target of jeers and sly remarks, even a comparison to make us feel better about ourselves, and in the end, the

scapegoat for all of our own unresolved fears and insecurities.

We looked at her as the failed Christian when really, we
all failed her. We failed to realize that there is no such thing
as a failed Christian, as it is impossible for us to fail God. It
wasn't our fault either. We were taught that a Christian was
someone who had successfully conditioned themselves to
meet a particular set of standards and thus been granted the
ability to join the family of believers and follow God. But
we didn't know that those standards were our church's and
not God's. God takes us where we are, no matter where that
is. And if anyone tries to tell you otherwise, they are trying
to recruit you to *their* cause, not God's.

Riley failed to meet our church's standards and was
shamed as if she was directly defying God's will. This is
outrageous because even if she were, that shame still
wouldn't be merited. For the majority of the first twenty
years of her life, she was viewed as the dangerous outcast, as
if God has not called us all into inclusion, into unity with
Him, into His home. Into His *family*. And because the entry
fee is absolutely nothing, we have no right to act as the
bouncer at the door, deciding who is good enough to come
inside.

So many of us constantly feel the need to audit every
person who desires to be a part of God's kingdom, as if we
are somehow qualified enough to be the ones to do so. Yet
the qualifications we place on the hopeful candidates are
always uncannily reminiscent of ourselves. They must
believe what *we* believe, live how *we* live, say what *we* say,
even *think* what *we* think. Then, and only then, do they get
to experience God with us. If they don't meet these
requirements, they are given two options. Either surrender
their "pride" and "sin" and conform to our ways of doing
things, or be denied God. Ultimately, we as a church end

up denying many more people of God than we lead to Him.

In her book *Searching For Sunday,* Rachel Held Evans expresses a similar view. "Evangelicalism in particular has seen a resurgence of border patrol Christianity… which declares anyone who fails to conform to their strict set of beliefs and behaviors unfit for Christian fellowship. Committed to purifying the church of every errant thought, difference of opinion, or variation in practice, these self-appointed gatekeepers tie up heavy loads of legalistic rules and place them on weary people's shoulders… But the gospel doesn't need a coalition devoted to keeping the wrong people out. It needs a family of sinners, saved by grace, committed to tearing down the walls, throwing open the doors, and shouting 'Welcome! There's bread and wine. Come eat with us and talk.' This isn't a kingdom for the worthy; it's a kingdom for the hungry."

We can't be the ones blocking the door to God. The world has plenty of those already. What we should be, all God needs us to be, are the ones holding the door open as wide as possible with one hand and ushering in any and every soul we see with the other. They don't have to be anything more than who they are.

Imagine if this is what Riley was told at the very beginning, that she didn't have to be someone else to be loved by God *completely.* That there was nothing wrong with her and that no matter what, the people put around her by God would stick by her side to prove that His love is infinite and unending. That she wasn't broken. In fact, she wasn't even damaged. She was created by God exactly how she was so that God would be able to know her deeply and intimately, and that she might do the same.

There is a common idea shared among many churches and religious communities that we are broken by default, but through us finding and knowing God can be fixed. Though I understand the sentiment of God being the one who picks us up and pulls us together, I do not believe that we start off broken. God does not make mistakes. He *cannot* make mistakes. He made each and every one of us intentionally and exactly. He made you perfectly. You are made to be imperfect, yes, so that we can discern true perfection that is only found in God. But you are not inherently defective.

We are not broken. We are simply incomplete. And because we are not broken, God does not fix us. He *fills* us. He fills the emptiness in our hearts. He fills the void in our souls. Without God, we are not damaged. We are not valueless. We are extremely valuable, both to others and to God, whether we know God or not. However, it is only through a relationship with Him that we can truly understand just how valuable we really are.

11

A CULTURE OF CONDEMNATION

During my freshman year of college, I was approached by a very close friend of mine, one of my best friends at the time, who shared that he wanted to have a conversation with me and one of the leaders of the teen ministry, who had been the one to lead us both through our Bible studies and baptize us. The reasoning was a bit vague, but at the time, he and I were a bit distant due to some disagreements. Naturally, I assumed this talk was to help us work through the complication. His friendship was really important to me, so of course I agreed to the conversation.

It ended up taking over a month for the talk to actually happen. It seemed his urgency to have it had dwindled, so I took it upon myself to contact my friend and the leader to ensure it happened. The sooner we could all talk, the sooner we could mend the relationship, which was my highest priority.

Finally, after weeks, we found a day to meet at the leader's house, and within five minutes of us sitting down at the table on his back patio, I was made aware of the real reason for the meeting. It turned out, it was not to help work through the complications of our own friendship. As my friend revealed to the leader and me for the first time, the reason he wanted to talk was because he felt that I was spending too much time with the girl I liked. To be clear, this was during the period just after our nearly two-year-long texting ban had been "lifted," and we were finally becoming more confident in being around each other.

My friend had not voiced his concern to me before this exact moment. He hadn't talked to me about it at all, not until we were in the witness of someone who had "authority." I felt cornered. Betrayed. He knew I was already on thin ice with these leaders after everything that had happened, as it was no secret that not everyone felt as good about how it concluded as I did.

This friend and I had known each other since elementary school and had been best friends for nearly the same amount of time. And now, here he was, denouncing me and my actions in front of someone else, a church leader no less, without me having even the faintest idea he had any adverse feelings about it. He used my vulnerability to his advantage, keeping me in the dark until there was no way out, to what gain I still did not know.

I barely had time to keep up with the conversation as the accusations began to fly, as I was still trying to come to terms with the curveball that I had been thrown, let alone the time to come up with answers to defend myself against them. So, for over an hour, I sat on one side of the table while my best friend and closest teen leader sat across from me, saying whatever my panicked mind could come up with, but already defeated and knowing it didn't matter *what* I said.

Many things were said during our talk, but surprisingly, among all the allegations and hurt feelings, the thing I remember most was a single line directed at my friend and me, surprisingly spoken by the youth leader rather than my friend. As we talked, he casually started a sentence by explaining, "Well, you both have bad boundaries with girls..." I honestly don't remember the rest of the sentence because the remark caught me off guard. This was the first time I had ever been confronted with the idea that I was looked at as someone who had bad boundaries with girls, as a general idea.

Of course, I knew that there were many people with a lot of different perspectives on how this girl and I had gone about our situation, based on the previous false rumor that we had "crossed boundaries" a ways back after we had gone on a date with the full support of our parents. And now here I was, at a teen leader's house per the request of my friend, whose only reason was to try and out me because he didn't like that this girl and I were spending time together. But this was the first time I had realized that this was now how some people seemed to view me.

It was a shock. And it hurt, because I felt that it was completely false and unjustified. It hurt because for all my years as a Christian, I had been trying my absolute hardest to live my life in as much of a God-honoring way as possible, yet I was still regarded as someone who had failed. But looking back, it hurt the most because, when this church leader said it, it wasn't even the point of his statement. It was just the beginning of the sentence. It was before the comma. It was said in passing, as if it was common knowledge, and used as the basis for whatever he actually intended to say. In response, I remember laying my hands on the table in front of me and telling them, "With all due respect, I disagree." If it wasn't possible to change their minds at this point, it was at least worth it to voice what I believed.

The idea that this was some core truth about me that

people just regarded as who I was, more than anything else, made me feel as if nothing else that I did mattered. It didn't matter how hard I tried. It didn't matter what my intentions were. It didn't even matter that I had never even gone so far as to hold a girl's hand in my entire life. It only mattered that a few people perceived my actions as holding bad boundaries, and now it was permanently attached to me.

So here I was, having been away at college, and asked by one of my best friends to come back on a weekend to talk with this youth leader present... never mentioning to me the real reason why he wanted to talk until we were face to face with no way out. And it turned out that all he wanted to do was tell our youth leader and me that he thought I was spending too much time with this girl.

Now, for any issue (never mind some crazy legalistic "concern" like this), one would think that the youth leader's first response would be to ask whether or not the friend had spoken directly to me about his concerns first, and suggest he have a conversation with me first to express his thoughts. But that never happened.

And it didn't end there. When the meeting was nearing its end, my friend suddenly said he needed to go because his "Uber was here." The weird thing was, I had never seen him pull out his phone to order the Uber in the first place, yet he was now letting us know that it was pulling up out front.

He quickly got up from the table and made his way to the front door, surely not realizing that the youth leader and I were going to get up and walk him out. The leader may have been doing it out of courtesy, but I was already suspicious and wanted to see what awaited us outside. Though I already had a slight idea.

We all walked out the front door, where no car waited. The friend quickly said his goodbyes and made a beeline down the street, where several houses down, I could see that his "Uber" wasn't an Uber at all, but the car of the girl that he was accusing me of spending too much time with. The girl who this entire gathering was about. My friend, a bit frazzled, got in the car, and it sped off, leaving me out of words.

Curious, I turned to the youth leader, certain he had perceived what had happened. Maybe it was too much to hope for some sort of acknowledgment of the utter absurdity of the whole thing. I could tell he had seen it too. He had put the pieces together. Yet, when I turned to him, he simply gave me a grin, said goodbye, and walked back inside.

* * *

Christianity has a problem with labels. Wait. Let me back up. Humanity as a whole has a problem with labels. But as Christians, we have held onto these superficial designations for some reason when we should be the group of people who most understand how untrue they are. By labels, I am referring to people being known by one or two primary aspects of their character or things they have done.

It's not always a bad thing. We see our neighbor as the person who brought over soup when we were sick. We see our brother or sister as the one who can always tell when we aren't feeling ourselves. But for some reason, sadly, it's the negative things that tend to overstay their welcome in our minds. Steve is the one who started the rumor about you that made everyone distance themselves from you in high school. Erica tried to steal your phone when you left it at her house last year. And on and on. Forgiveness is a vital aspect of this dynamic, which helps us move on from these conditions. But many of us get stuck here, unable to let the past go and forever seeing people as a culmination of the things that they have done.

Forgiveness takes on a much different meaning when you bring God into the picture. It is no longer a service you offer to someone if you so choose out of the kindness of your heart who may or may not deserve it. It is now a gift given to everyone by Jesus, putting us all in the same boat of the undeserving.

None of us are worthy, yet all of us are forgiven. Forgiveness from one person to another is now no longer seen as something that can be offered, but something that would be wrong to deny. It is not what frees the other person if granted, but the thing that will keep us entangled if withheld. And above all, we know that because of the forgiveness gifted to us by God, we are not defined by anything done in our past, but solely by the one who has forgiven us.

As Christians we know this. As churches, we preach this. Yet, in so many scenarios, we continue to view the people around us as the sum of their shortcomings rather than their wholeness in Christ. Despite the fact that we are all made new in Jesus, that person is still viewed as the alcoholic and that person as the addict. That person has anger issues, that one is a bad influence, and that one is weak in their faith and will never be able to play an essential role in the church's ecosystem. That person left the church for a while, so you can never know where their heart is truly at. That person used to lie all the time and can never be trusted. The list goes on indefinitely.

Yet, in these scenarios, I am describing people who no longer subscribe to those elements of themselves that they used to feed into. They have given themselves over to God and allowed Jesus and the Holy Spirit to change them, to transform them into new creations. We know this. But why do we still label them?

It's because, at our core, we don't believe it. We don't truly believe for a one hundred percent fact that God has changed us. Some of us are stuck at wondering if He even has the power to do so, while others doubt that His power indeed did its job on that person. If we did believe it completely, we would no longer see someone as the sum of their most incriminating characteristics. We would know that they are free, just as free as we are and, therefore, no longer have to answer to the parts of them that Jesus took to the cross with Him.

Do people still fall back into the rhythms that used to define them before being transformed by Christ? Yes. All the time. Think about who you were before turning your life over to God. Were you a liar? An addict? A coward? After giving up those parts of you and accepting Jesus' offer to leave them behind, there are still moments every day where those parts of us whisper in our ears, echoes of the past that offer fleeting temptations. We now have the power to deny them and say no. We can now choose Jesus. But that doesn't mean we always do. Even so, we are now no longer defined by those things. Jesus has stripped the name tag off your shirt that says things such as "Liar," "Cheater," and "Hopeless" and replaced it with one that says "Mine."

Jesus is who defines each and every one of us. That doesn't make us Jesus. If that were the case, that's the name that would be on our name tag. But it isn't. We are still our own people who have our own battles and struggles. But we belong to Him. And in Him is where we find our identity. We can no longer look at people as who they once were because it simply isn't who they are anymore. They are Jesus'. And so are you.

Untruth: You Are Defined By What You Do
Truth: You Are Defined By What Jesus Did

A prominent portion of the culture around Christianity has been erected around the idea that we having to "qualify" for acceptance, and has resulted in a measureless amount of people being terrified at the thought of falling short of God's grace (which the Bible makes clear we ALL have, and it's okay—Romans 3:23). When it is revealed that someone has done something wrong, or simply gone against the status quo, shame is imposed upon them because everyone around them is desperately trying to be infallible, and that person no longer fits in, or may even be seen as holding everyone else down. This perfectionist culture is so incredibly harmful because that idea is the opposite of what scripture tells us.

One of the most important verses in the Bible is the opening line of Romans 8. I know, I know, all scripture is created equal. But be honest with yourself; there are a handful of scriptures that just hit a little harder than others. This is one of them. The first two verses of the chapter say, "Therefore, there is now no condemnation for those who are in Christ Jesus, because through Christ Jesus the law of the Spirit who gives life has set you free from the law of sin and death." Mind. Blown. The directness and definitiveness of the Bible cannot be understated. There is no dabbling around the issues and questions. God doesn't waste any time giving us exactly what we need to hear.

There is **NO CONDEMNATION** for those who are in Christ Jesus. This means anyone who follows God and believes that Jesus is who He says He is and did what the Bible says He did will not and cannot *ever* be condemned.

Just to lay it out, condemnation is a sentencing. Just as one who commits a felony is sentenced to jail, one who is condemned is declared guilty and punished disapprovingly. Do we do things that deserve disapproval every day? Heck yes we do. Do we deserve to be condemned? Absolutely. But because Jesus bore that condemnation in its entirety, we won't be. Ever.

Many Christians' understanding of this verse has devolved to a level on which the clarity of its message evades them, and is replaced by nuance, which this verse is devoid of entirely. Even when we say we believe it, how we deal with other people shows that we don't, at least not entirely, as there is still a rampant amount of condemnation being issued on a regular basis, sadly often more so by Christians than anyone else. And if this condemnation is not coming from God, which He tells us it isn't, then there are only two other places it can be coming from: other people and ourselves. If God has proclaimed that He will not condemn us, what makes us believe we have the right to do so on His behalf?

The idea that we are free from any and all condemnation is yet another truth that has been declared clearly and absolutely, yet is not always fully believed. If we are not completely assured that God will never condemn us, then we will begin accepting the condemning actions of others or even become the condemners ourselves. Out of what we perceive to be love, we will start implementing rules, boundaries, and practices to constrain people in an effort to stop any action that could be condemnable from happening. That's what happened in my church and what I know happens in so many others. But as we've seen, that simply does not work.

Untruth: More Rules = Less Room For Mistakes
Truth: More Rules = Less Room For God

In the life of a believer, rules such as these do nothing but promote the lifestyle of that which they attempt to inhibit. God has set forth a certain number of commandments for us, which we are to strive to attain and live by. But the plethora of superfluous rules we have added and allowed to shape our lives and spiritual communities have only damaged and reinforced the notion that we aren't fully confident of our complete freedom from condemnation. And to those on the receiving end of said condemnation, who aren't assured of this truth, there is only one belief to gain: if other followers of God condemn me, then God must condemn me as well.

* * *

If you grew up in church or have been in one long enough to witness people you know leave, how did your church handle it?

Some churches are great about it because they recognize that they are not the end-all-be-all in that person's life, and God has a destiny and plan for everyone. In my church growing up, the mentality was unfortunately quite different and, resultantly, passed some pretty twisted views onto my friends and me when we were younger.

When someone decided to leave our church, for whatever reason, it suddenly didn't matter who they were or how they were regarded while they were a member. They may have been a part of our church for decades. They might have been a ministry leader, or a member of the worship team, or simply a highly respected friend and peer. It didn't matter. According to many of those in leadership positions, once they decided to leave, it was because they were misled, prideful, arrogant, and drifting from God. I knew many people growing up who ended up leaving our church, and there wasn't a single person to my knowledge who was regarded as leaving for the "right reasons," whatever those reasons may be.

That's because there will never be a good enough reason if your church truly believes they are the only proper way to God. After a while, you have to think about that fact and ask yourself if it is actually true. Interestingly, the people leaving their ministry usually aren't even leaving the Church or Christianity as a whole. They are only leaving their specific church. In some cases, the only reason they left is that they were *moving* and would be too far to attend. Yet, regardless, they are spoken of and regarded as if they have disavowed God and abandoned their faith entirely.

Are you familiar with the term "falling away?" If not, it is often used to describe those who leave the church. You ask where someone has been the last couple weeks, and you'll be told off-handedly they fell away. No explanation. No further analysis. Done deal. It's almost as if they have died. It is an idea so definitive in its conclusion that there's usually nothing else to say. In many ways, that was how the people who decided to leave my church were regarded. As if they were dead. And the reason is that, to the church that they left, they might as well be.

Growing up, I witnessed plenty of people leave. Some I knew, some I didn't. Others I was pretty close to. I think about one person in particular, who was a friend of most everyone while they were a member. Though, once they left, they were suddenly the brunt of many passing jokes and passive statements in the youth ministry.

Back then, although it struck me as being in bad taste, what it *didn't* strike me as was inaccurate. They had left. And it was because they had fallen away from their faith. They had chosen the world over God. What I failed to realize was the fact that that's how it always seemed to be, every single time. There was never any alternative reasoning. It was always because they were weaker. It was always because they had failed.

One of the biggest lies a church can tell you is that they are the only way to God. That if you decide to leave, even to go to another church, you are choosing an inferior faith experience and therefore are not living in God's will. Our church generally believed this, and though if you asked the members, most would deny it, how the church worked at a structural level clearly demonstrated that this was their true belief.

If you want to know what someone truly thinks about something, don't listen to what they say. Observe what they do. I slowly began to understand this as I got older, and the people who were leaving were people I knew were just as firm in their faith as anyone else. Suddenly, being presented as falling away didn't sit right with me.

And then it happened to my family and me. Once we finally decided it was time for us to move on and do what was best for us, these things were said of us to members of our church when asked where we had gone. To those who inquired, we were prideful, arrogant, refused to listen to advice, and thus lost sight of God. Anything that would put the blame on the people leaving and take it away from anything that could possibly be wrong with the ecosystem that is causing those people to leave.

But my decision to leave my church wouldn't be made for nearly another two years. At this point, I was exhausted, overwhelmed by all the bits and pieces in my life that seemed to be becoming increasingly unstable. From rocky friendships to convoluted church politics, I needed to take a step back to figure out what I thought about it all, what to do next, and how to approach finding a solution. The perfect opportunity to do so presented itself in me leaving for college.

12

RUNNING ON EMPTY

To be fair, *leaving* for college may not be the most accurate term. That previous April, I had been accepted to attend the filmmaking program at UCLA, which, among being one of the top five highest-ranked film schools in the world, also happened to only be a twenty-minute drive from my house. But I wanted the full freshman experience, to immerse myself in the college culture, and honestly, to get as much "away" as I could given the circumstances at my church. So I opted to live in a dorm on campus.

For a while, it seemed to be helpful. Yes, I was living with two strangers to whom I rarely ever talked, one of whom never seemed to wear deodorant and created an eye-watering, eyebrow-singeing odor that engulfed the entire room for twenty-four hours a day. But, surprisingly, it was a breath of fresh air (well, maybe not literally) being able to take a step back and just breathe for a while.

However, it was short-lived. One of the things I was most excited about in this new stage of my life was the opportunity to experience an entirely new church ministry, and I was optimistic about what I might find there. But it didn't take long to realize that this new ministry I had joined was much the same as what I had hoped to be leaving behind.

* * *

When you're in college, something that immediately presents itself to you is just how many different kinds of people you find yourself around. People of every race and religion, who each think about the world in very different ways. The number of diverse backgrounds and perspectives is astounding. However, despite all of the distinctions within the student body, there is one thing many seem to have in common.

They like to *do* things.

I don't mean any arbitrary thing. I'm talking about things that matter. Things that will make waves. Things that will change the world.

When you're in college, you're the next generation. The up-and-comers. In baseball terms, you are on deck to be the next people whose thoughts and actions will dictate the future direction the world will take. And it starts here, in college.

Whatever campus you find yourself on, it is quite nearly impossible to walk from one end to the other without running into people with brochures and clipboards, booths set up by clubs and organizations for various interests and causes, and signs plastered on every bulletin and lamppost encouraging people to join, donate, or spread the word for some type of purpose.

Among these are the church campus ministry groups, or, in the case of UCLA, over 100 different church campus ministries, eagerly inviting people to show up to a weekly service or hop in a Bible study. From a conceptual standpoint, this is a pretty cool thing. To see such a presence of people trying to lead others to God is incredible. But, after having witnessed the intricacies of this environment for three years (my fourth year of college being spent on Zoom during Covid), the question that most frequently came to mind was, "What type of experience are we actually inviting these people into?"

It didn't take long for me to get my answer. What I said about college students liking to do things? The same is true with Christians. And in many cases it is far from healthy. That being said, when you have people who are both Christians *and* college students... Well, I think you can connect the dots.

During my time in the college church ministry, it quickly became clear just how wrapped up everyone seemed to be in *doing*. We had the typical Sunday service, sometimes with an extra group that met an hour earlier. There was a Friday night college devotional. There was a Wednesday night midweek devotional. On Tuesday or Thursday there was a student-led Bible group sometime during the day, and the other free day was usually reserved for a campus-specific hangout. Between these, there were scheduled time slots designated for "cold contact" sharing, where you would go out in pairs to reach out to as many people as you could on campus and try to convince them to show up to one of that week's get-togethers. And based on the particular week, there was an assortment of other activities, events, and outreach exercises.

Now, individually, are any of these things bad? Absolutely not. I want to make that clear. Each of these things are in and of themselves not only good but condoned, some even commanded, by God. They are the building blocks to a deep, healthy relationship with Him and your fellow friends in Christ, making it even more complicated to figure out how someone's participation in such events correlates to their devotion to Christ.

The schedule of a college student is already one of the most stressful and sleepless periods of time in their life, without the commitments to a church or religious group. I want to make sure I explain this with care, as I don't want it to sound like the obligations that come with a Christian life are just that... obligations. The things Christians do are, first and foremost, to grow closer to God, and help others do the same. Which is why, in my experience through college, it was a major point of contention with me that when students in our ministry couldn't make it to these events, they would be considered as not having their priorities straight.

I have no shame in saying that it didn't take me very long to find myself running on empty when trying to keep up with the rigidity of the campus ministry schedule. And to be frank, my film school obligations were considered much lighter on classes and homework than many other majors, yet I still found myself trying to keep my head above water.

I remember my first, and only, experience cold-contact sharing with the campus ministry, setting off around campus in pairs, scouring every hallway and bench like bloodthirsty predators for any unsuspecting student to devou- um, I mean "share our faith" with. It was always the ones by themselves, quietly studying or walking to class. They were the ones to go for, because the odds were, they were the ones most likely to be in need of community.

We must have approached a good six or seven people in the hour we were given before our campus midweek devotional. I was way out of my comfort zone, but luckily it wasn't my partner's first rodeo. She knew what to say, as well as the fastest way to get from being total strangers with someone to being able to invite them to the gathering later that evening. It was a science, really, and it went something like this:

"Hey there, what's your name?"

"Nice to meet you. My name is _____. Are you a student here?"

"Nice. What grade are you in?"

"Nice. What are you majoring in?"

"Nice. So random question, but are you religious at all?

"Nice. Well interestingly enough, we're a part of a Christian ministry on campus and are having a devotional later tonight. Would you be interested in joining us?"

If they answer "Yes"- *"Awesome! Give me your number and I'll text you the details."*

If they answer "No"- *"Oh, okay. Bye!"*

This was pretty much exactly how each one of those six or seven conversations went, give or take a few more formalities. I'm not even sure if "conversation" is the correct term. I think "interview" would be a more accurate description. *Nice. Nice. Nice. Uhu, nice. Oh, nice....*

Aaaaaaanyway...

The goal was to break as much ice as possible in thirty seconds to get to the real reason we were actually there interrupting you while you were trying to study for your midterm. And in the process, completely forgetting any piece of information you told us other than your name, on a good day. In one ear and out the other. And the reason is that we aren't there to get to know these people. We aren't there to make friends. We're there to satisfy a quota. And despite all the excuses about how "we're the ones with something to offer, and it's our privilege and mission to share what we have with others," we're not serving them.

We're not there because of what we have to offer them, no matter how deeply we believe it. We are there, in that moment, because they have something to offer *us*, whether they know it or not.

At that moment, they are not a soul desperate for the very thing we happen to have. They are simply a number that we can add to our ranks. An outcast that we can sell on community. A branch of influence into a different demographic of people for us to spread our reach. A wallet that can contribute to the funding of our cause. We know this because if they were anything more to us than this, the conversation wouldn't be over the second they declined our invitation.

As if it needed to be pointed out, Jesus never cared about the *quantity* of people following Him. As a matter of fact, there were instances where He asked those whom He performed miracles for to keep quiet about it so that He could stay on the down low. What He cared about was the *quality* of the relationships He had with each and every person who knew Him. He not only wanted people to know Him as truly and intimately as possible, but He also had a profound and authentic desire to know them as well.

If you were to go through the Bible and recount all of the interactions Jesus had with people, you would be astounded by how many of them decided to follow Him solely due to His genuine interest in them. More than them being told they needed to know and follow Jesus, what turned their heart was the realization that someone actually desired to know *them,* with no strings attached.

Christianity is not about seeing how many people we can get to follow God. Even though seeing an entire generation turned to Christ sounds like the ideal end goal, it is not, nor has it ever been, about the numbers. More than anything else, over any other cause or mission or purpose,

Christianity is and needs to be about love. Not love *if*, not love *when*. Just love. People need to be treated not as potential applicants for the position of "Christ Follower", but as beings who are desperately in need of love. Not only can we then provide them with our love, we can also show them a love that is boundless and never-ending. We have precisely what they're looking for, and we can give it to them without any fear of it running out. Trust me; if this is how Christians approached every interaction with the people they came across every day, an entire generation *would* be turned to Christ.

We are not sent to accumulate people. We are sent to love them. We have to stop viewing people as projects and start viewing them as souls. Every soul is invaluable; if we truly understood that, our interest in someone wouldn't dwindle when they say they can't be our plus one to church. We would just love them.

Of course, I didn't grasp all of this at the time. At the moment, it all just felt off to me, like we were missing a crucial element, a *human* element. And in its place, we had a production element, like a factory or an assembly line. It didn't feel authentic, and everybody saw right through it.

Unsurprisingly, no one accepted our invitation that day.

* * *

If so many scriptures paint a picture of complete peace, joy, and rest in God's love and grace, why is it that the majority of Christians seem to be running on empty as they attempt to complete an endless list of tasks to satisfy God's will? The definition of work, according to the dictionary, is "activity involving mental or physical effort done in order to achieve a purpose or result."

Everything we do, we do for a purpose—a desired

outcome or result. The work God wants us to do is what the Holy Spirit leads us to do on a moment-to-moment basis. This work will only lead to satisfaction, peace, and prosperity. But so much of Christian culture has instead opted for a dynamic of labor grounded in deprivation.

We work out of fear rather than faith. We are afraid that, should we not live up to the expectations of God, we will be rejected and denied His grace and salvation. And for those who may not hold such stark notions, there is in many a simple fear of being rejected by the church, proving that they are the weak link, the one whose faith is faltering when everyone else's seems to be steadfast.

There is a reason God created us as human *beings* and not human *doings*. He wants us to "be". Be with Him. Be *in* Him, as John 15:4 emphasizes when Jesus implores us to "Remain in me, as I also remain in you. No branch can bear fruit by itself; it must remain in the vine. Neither can you bear fruit unless you remain in me." We were created for one sole reason: to be with God. Of course, the drive set in our hearts is to accomplish fantastic things, but those things do not come to fruition by us setting off on where we "assume" God would want us to go and do what we think God would want us to do.

You may be familiar with the idea of "Doing great things for God." It sounds great. Noble. But when you think about the fact that we are incapable of doing anything on our own, the absurdity of assuming we can actually do anything *for* God begins to present itself. God does not need us. There is no simpler way to say it. There is not one thing that our existence does to assist, increase, or enhance anything that God cannot already do on His own. He does not need us for any work or mission that He desires to be achieved in this world.

But he *wants* us. He wants us to be a part of the wonders

that He sets into motion. He has created us to take part in His endeavors because He wants us to be able to experience Him. It is not about the work we are doing. It never has been, and it never will be. If He genuinely needs something to happen or be done, it will be, no matter how greatly we fail or succeed in our role in it. And no matter how hard we try to make something happen, if God determines that it should not be, it won't.

No matter how wrapped up we get in the "mission" or the "good work" or how "fruitful" our endeavors are, it simply does not matter if it is not done *with God*.

The point isn't to do great things for God. It is to be with God.

The point isn't to save people. It is to be with God.

The point isn't to know your Bible from cover to cover. It is to be with God.

The point isn't to stop sinning. It is to be with God.

The point isn't even to make disciples. It is to be with God.

If we settle for making any of these subsidiary pursuits our life's primary purpose, we will never experience God as fully as He has created us to. But if we strive to be with God in everything we do, then everything we do will be exactly what is desired of us. Will it look different for each of us? Absolutely. But no matter what it is that we find ourselves doing, we are united in the fact that it will pale in comparison to how closely we are communing with Christ.

> **Untruth:** *God Calls Us to Do*
> **Truth:** *God Calls Us to Be*

For most of my freshman year of college, I struggled to find the balance between what I felt was good for me to be doing with the campus ministry and what was only making things more difficult. It occurred to me very early on that what it would take to accurately achieve the perception of a "spiritually mature and stable Christ follower" was far more than I felt I had the capacity for, especially in the current place I was in in my spiritual walk.

I had been dealing with so much in my church life those last few months, years really, that what I needed more than anything was a safe place to rest my head, surrounded by people whom I didn't have to prove myself to, who weren't connected to anything I was dealing with, and be refreshed and reinvigorated. Instead, I was presented with a brand new obstacle course to traverse, with even more obligations and commitments than before.

I gave it my all for several months because I wanted people to know that I cared. But it was a demeanor I couldn't keep up. For my sophomore year, I ditched dorm life and agreed to share an apartment with three guys from the campus ministry, none of whom I had met before, as they were all new to UCLA that year. I was excited at the prospect of being able to have these potential new friends to be that place of rest and community I had been yearning for. Unfortunately, it wasn't far from being just the opposite.

By the end of the previous school year, I had simply begun to slow down. I didn't have it in me. I knew I was at my max. To be honest, I had already hit my max *before* I left for college, but now I knew I had to take my foot off the gas. However, now that I was rooming with other members of the ministry, the pressure to show up was always present. I dreaded the moment that always came before my roommates left for a church event, where the question would be posed in a quiet, glaring manner if in fact everyone was planning on going. There was an unvoiced assumption that, unless someone in your family was in the hospital, the answer would be "yes."

Until there was the first "no." On this particular evening, my roommates had left for our ministry's midweek devotional at different times. After some deliberation and a few prior conversations with my parents on the phone, I decided that that night would be the night I decided to stay home, which I shared with two of my roommates before they left. Surprisingly, it was a much bigger decision than people may assume. Growing up in a church environment with a similar expectation, I knew that my actions would warrant a response in some form or fashion. I just didn't know when, or how.

What I didn't expect was a phone call less than an hour later, *during* the ministry devotional, from the *one* roommate who hadn't been home when I had shared that I was staying back, asking where I was.

Immediately, this didn't register as the call one might get from someone who was genuinely curious about where they were, or perhaps wanted to make sure they were okay. Because it wasn't that type of call. It was an expectant call, where they didn't care where I was or how I was, but only that I wasn't *there*. I didn't have some crazy excuse or other obligation that rendered me unable to attend. But I was tired, and doing what was best for me, which was staying in and reading that night. And that's what I told him.

Big mistake. From that moment, I felt a tangible shift in others' perception of me in the campus ministry. Not from everyone, of course. At the end of the day, most of the people I met there were good people, and many truly loved God. But my "image" was now not of someone who could potentially be a leader in the ministry, but of someone who was weaker in their faith and needed to be watched and pushed to make sure they stayed on the straight and narrow. All of the intentional work I had put in during the entirety of my freshman year in an effort to showcase that I was authentic about my faith was now reduced to rubble over one missed devotional for which I had no admissible excuse.

It wasn't even a week later that, while I was in my room studying, this same roommate barged in unannounced and decreed to me that he had had a conversation with the head pastor of the church (without my knowledge), and the pastor had granted him the authority to be my "discipler."

Maybe you are familiar with this term. If not, good for you. Because while the term is displayed as someone who acts as a mentor, accountability partner, and the like, in many scenarios, they are simply appointed to keep a rein on people they feel are at risk of leaving, or at least making decisions they don't like. Remember one of the categories of spiritual abuse? Enforced Accountability.

To be clear, the *role* of a discipler can be good, when that person is older and wiser and can offer wisdom and advice when sought… and if you *choose* to want them in your life. But, many times, disciplers are used as leashes to rein people in and are provided to people despite their wishes when leaders deem them weaker in their faith.

Now, without my consent in the matter, there was a kid, the same age as me, who, if we're really splitting hairs, had only been a part of the church a fraction of the time I had, who had been given spiritual authority over me by the head of the church to keep me in line because I missed one single church gathering that week. Plus, I had only known this guy for a few months, and at that time had never even had a conversation with the head pastor ever. He didn't know who I was, only that I didn't show up to a devotional even though I could have. And now they wanted to make sure I never missed another.

How'd that go, you ask? Well, in true submissive form, I went from *missing* one devotional a week to not even *showing up* to one devotional a week. I'm sure that was the intended result. But I had had it. Missing that first devotional was a trial run, dipping my toe in the water and testing how things went. And the answer I got was clear.

I knew who I was and, more importantly, who God was. And while these truly good, God-loving people were trying their hardest to *do* these things for God, the result was *just not Him.* At the end of the day, the scale of someone's faith and convictions were dictated not by their heart but by their actions. By their attendance record. And the result was a superficial and shallow church experience.

I don't say these things to build me up in any way, but because one of the saddest things about all of this was all of the people during the two or so years I was a part of that campus ministry who didn't have the roots that I had been fortunate enough to develop from my parents and home life outside of church, who I saw come and go, come and go, come and go. Friends who agreed to show up to a devo or hang out night. Students who were met and invited on campus who in their hearts knew something was missing in their lives, and felt some sort of spark that told them that this might be it.

So they show up and meet many of these warm, happy, godly people. It feels… right. They come to a Sunday service and hear the word of God for maybe the first time, and it's a feeling they've never experienced before. Their eyes are opened, and there is a spring in their step. Before long, they can't get enough of the wealth flowing from God's word and the riches of Jesus' love and grace.

But then they have to miss a week because they have to finish a project for class. And when they come back, there's this… tension? Apprehension? They can't quite put a finger on it. But the lesson is still good; the words spoken still fill their soul.

They can't make it to the midweek on Wednesday because they have soccer practice. They wish they could be there, they *want* to be there, but they can't be. When they show up the next Sunday, they get stopped by the pastor, who speaks with them about their priorities. To him, it seems they aren't as devoted as they could be. As they *should* be. They don't know how to react to this. Maybe he's right. Perhaps they're not doing enough.

Now they feel shame. A shame they didn't even know they could feel. So they try to make it work, but no matter what they do, they are upsetting someone in their life. The only difference is that the people at church are the only ones who make the failure feel like it's coming from *inside* them, a result of who they are rather than their circumstances.

Soon, it doesn't matter how the lessons make them feel. It's not worth it. Because for every positive thing Jesus makes them feel, it is equaled by the weight placed on them by the other people in the church. So they leave. Because according to those around them, this is God. And if this is God, why would they want anything to do with Him?

The saddest part is that when these people leave, often never to be heard from again, we reason that they simply weren't spiritual enough. They weren't strong enough. We say that the weight and pull of the world were too strong for them, and they chose those things over God. But what God are we showing them?

In only that short time in the campus ministry, I witnessed way too many people come and go in a similar fashion. While some left just as quickly as they came, others stuck around for a while. Some stayed months, others a year or two. Those people, the ones that actually tried and gave their time and their hearts, are the ones I feel for the most. Because their pain was deeper, and their decision to leave had much longer-lasting effects. They invested, and in the end, those investments felt like a waste.

Will these people ever give God a chance again? Only He knows. I hope so. But for many, not just for our campus ministry but for churches worldwide, this was the one time they will ever be so closely exposed to Christ. And because of the misrepresentation given by those whose only job is to show them the true Christ, they will never give Him another chance.

Now, there are others, and several whom I have met, who left because they knew that what they were experiencing wasn't the fullness of God. God was there, of course. I don't want to make it sound like He wasn't. But He wasn't there *fully*. It wasn't Him in completeness, but aspects of Him. An outline, filled in with other superfluous things that only ended up distracting people or pushing them away. These people left because they knew there was more.

You may be asking, "Why not stay and help show these people the fullness of God instead of leaving?" After all, it's not everyone else's job to build you up without you being able to provide the same for others. That was my original mindset too, and it was and still is true.

However, in certain situations, you come to realize that people don't always want to compromise the way they do things, even if it would mean being able to take part in something better.

13

A FINAL STAND

There is almost always a time before deciding to leave a problematic situation where you first try to help bring about a solution. This was where I turned first, having the inspiration to try to give the students in the campus ministry some pieces of truth about God's grace and freedom. I wanted to help show them how few strings are attached to the gifts God gives us (spoiler alert, there aren't any).

For this reason, I decided to ask about leading one of the weekly small group devotionals with just the UCLA students. I was given the okay, and that week was able to talk to my peers about these foundational truths that I so badly wanted them to know.

Now, they already knew these things, as most of us do. We all "know" that God's love is unconditional. We all "know" His grace is unequivocal, cannot be earned, and thus can never be taken away. We are told these things repeatedly in every sermon, worship song, and inspirational Instagram post. But it would amaze you how few of us believe them at such a core level that we actually live as if they were true. And the reason for that is because the truth is so unbelievably in our favor that many of us can't fathom it. When the drone of day-to-day life causes these truths to drift to the back of our minds, the sheer enormity of them fades, and the lies of all the other voices around us drown them out, convincing us that they are too good to be true and that there must be a catch.

I knew that these people, who had all committed themselves to dedicated relationships with God, "knew" these things. But I wanted to offer them the facts again, from a perspective that highlighted that some of the ways we have turned to in our living out of these truths were not in line with the truths themselves. I presented them with a handful of scriptures directly addressing these promises, and I felt like the conversation went great.

At least, until it was over.

Our group dispersed, and I was approached by one of my roommates, my "discipler," who asked to speak with me. He didn't have anything to say about the lesson's content or thank me for sharing what was on my heart. The two things he had to say? First, apparently I used too many scriptures. And second, he recommended I stick to focusing on things like evangelism in my lessons and avoid talking about the Holy Spirit because it can tend to "go over people's heads."

Up until this point, it hadn't been entirely evident just how systematic the structure of the ministry was in its nature. But now, I could see that, in many ways, the authenticity so heavily needed for a genuine connection to God had been compromised in exchange for a much more regulatory and calculated approach to how everything operated. In this case, I am speaking of the ministry as a whole. On an individual basis, I can think of many members whose desire for God and approach to seeking Him did seem authentic. In such cases, it was even more of a disappointment to see their faith subjected to the confines of such a religiously rigid environment.

These young people enter college with a deep desire, a thirst, for God. And at first, the breath of fresh air that naturally accompanies that leap into the collegiate lifestyle feels like the absolute freedom to be able to express that desire and run wild with it. Like a snowball rolling down a hill, the motivation is there to simply let the energy move you, gaining momentum and attracting the people around you as you set off on your conquest for God.

The problem is that, soon enough, lines are placed in the sand, strategically, mind you, to expedite the process of bringing new people into the fold, and keeping them there. And I get it. It makes sense, at least from an organizational perspective.

At some point, way early on in the foundational days of such a ministry, someone decided to implement certain customs and practices out of the belief that they were necessary to ensure an environment that would promote the healthy growth of the ministry as a whole. But it doesn't work this way with a church. It can't, because when a church is treated as a business or regular organization, the members, at some point, begin to be treated as numbers rather than individual followers of God. Of course, it is rarely an intentional consequence.

In many of the churches or religious groups in which this happens, it is the result of actions made because its leaders genuinely wanted to bring as many people to Jesus as possible. But because of an unintentional negligence of the most significant factor in this entire equation, which is the authenticity necessary for a genuine relationship to form, there is a slow descent in the direction of legalistic mentalities and stringent practices that only further estrange people from that authenticity that is so imperative.

Soon enough, everyone is simply following procedures in what they do, say, and even think concerning God and what their purpose is on a day-to-day basis. Instead of a relational dynamic in which the members are encouraged and given the tools to be able to be led by God, through the Holy Spirit in how their relationship with Him grows and develops, the adherence to the ministry's manufactured methodologies becomes the only component by which the overall spiritual health of the ministry and its members is gauged. In other words, it's not about how well you feel your relationship with God is going, but rather how well you are adhering to the practices, ideas, and rules of your church ministry.

For those who have been able to build solid and authentic foundations in their relationship with God by themselves, hopefully the compulsion of such an environment does not end up encroaching on and muddling those healthy principles. But for those whose only connection to Christ has been through this type of church system, it quickly becomes an increasingly difficult task to differentiate it from an organic, unfettered relationship with God.

> **Untruth:** *The Key to God's Approval is Dedication*
> *to the Church*
> **Truth:** *The Key to God's Approval is Relationship*
> *with Christ*

So here I was, for the first time really understanding just how deeply ingrained these mentalities were in this ministry. Being in the space I was at the time, already dealing with an overwhelming amount of personal and spiritual turmoil from my home church, I didn't have the energy or willingness to try my luck at sticking it out and seeing what might be done. From what I could tell, I was attempting to do just that, and was being reprimanded for using too many scriptures in my devotional.

By the way, I used four scriptures in the entire lesson.

Four.

A couple of days after this, I had another conversation with my "discipler" about what he had to say, as it still didn't sit well with me. It didn't go well. By the end, my reasonings had been thrown to the curb, and the notion that kept being thrown at me was that my discipler didn't want me to "lose my treasure in Heaven." Lose my treasure in Heaven... For what? Using four scriptures in a Bible lesson? Or due to my resistance to the flow of the ministry? Either way, it felt like an awfully drastic jump in rationale.

To be honest, I wasn't then and am still not entirely sure what he was referring to by my "treasure in Heaven." I doubt he would've had a satisfying answer at the time either. Was he implying that if I continued to push against the boundary line of the church's structure, I was at risk of losing my salvation? That any act of not only direct rebellion but even slight contention against the way things were being done was equal to complete defiance of God himself, and as punishment, He would revoke the blessing of His grace on me? Perhaps a more probable answer was that his words weren't spoken in defense of God or the Church, but rather his own authority, which he felt was being threatened by my inherent questioning of it. Either way, I was astounded that an idea like that was actually verbalized, especially in a scenario so minor.

I didn't buy into the veiled threat; however, after that conversation, I stopped trying. For all intents and purposes, I was done with the campus ministry. I still had friends who were a part of that group and still do. But I was done with the system that I now understood it to be. And it wasn't just because I was tired of it all; I was also learning that it was starting to affect me in other ways.

* * *

Around that same time, I had gone home for a holiday break and attended a midweek service at my home church. I hadn't been back in several months, and since then, the situations that I had stepped away from when I left had come to a climax.

The issues between my two closest friends and me, ending with the "Uber" incident at our youth leader's house, had resulted in a complete falling out, evolving slowly over months of conversations at coffee shops and phone calls attempting to unearth whatever had lodged itself between us. Every conversation came up empty, and I couldn't figure out why. In the end, it turned out that I was being lied to, and the confrontation that ensued resulted in me being used as the scapegoat and ostracized from our friend group.

My main group of friends looked at me as an outsider, I was no longer on speaking terms with the girl I had liked and failed at developing a relationship with for the past four years, and the baggage and detritus of that whole experience lingered over me still. I felt like nearly everyone around me, both kids and adults, leaders and parents, looked at me differently because of it. And while that effect was surely exaggerated in my head, it had already been proven that a good portion of it was valid. What was once my safe haven was now a nearly foreign land.

I remember arriving at that midweek a little early, as people were hanging out in the main room before everything started. I felt off, like I didn't belong there. The room was full of people I knew, friends, but I couldn't shake the discomfort. As I entered the building and saw everyone in the main room, I couldn't even walk in, so I turned the corner, went into the single occupant bathroom, locked the door, and stayed there for over fifteen minutes.

My heart was racing, and no matter what I thought, I couldn't get myself to open the door and walk into the congregation. This was the church I had grown up in. I was born into it. Many of the people there were my longest and closest friends and peers, some who I would even consider my family. But that night, at that moment, it all felt alien to me, and I couldn't have felt more distant and unwelcome.

No part of me wanted to be there, and now here I was, hiding in the bathroom. Up to this point, I had never experienced anything like this. I wasn't a naturally anxious person, and this was the first time I ever recall feeling overwhelmed simply by being around other people. But it wasn't the last.

Within the same few weeks, my roommates and I were hosting a devotional at our apartment. All of the UCLA ministry members were there, and we were starting our Bible study. From what I remember, nothing about the contents of our discussion triggered any reaction from me. Honestly, I think it was just the fact that I was now attuned to the reality of what a get together like this actually was, and attributed it to many of the systemic issues that I was experiencing. As we all sat together, I felt my heartbeat quicken and the voices in the room start to fade.

I excused myself from the gathering and went into my bedroom, where I turned on the sink at the bathroom mirror and stuck my hands under the warm water. A similar situation occurred then, where I couldn't find it in myself to open the door and walk back out to the living room. It felt as if my feet were cemented to the floor, my body completely frozen in its place. So I stood there, my hands under the running water, until the time eventually came when I was able to take a breath and return to the group. If there was any doubt that the environment I was in was unhealthy for me, it dissipated with those two incidents. As it turns out, I wasn't the only one coming to these conclusions.

* * *

During the previous summer of my freshman year, my family hosted a "Back From College" group every week for our church's young adult/college ministry, where students would come to hang out, eat, and talk about their experiences in college and different ministries. We had friends who had gone to many different schools and church ministries all over the country, and we were hopeful to hear how they had been faring.

Sadly, from their stories and accounts, nearly every single one of them was having the same types of issues. False ideologies, rampant legalism, and ostracizing and shaming of people who were insistent on sticking to their convictions when presented with ideas that they didn't think aligned with God's word.

One friend recalled being pulled aside by the campus leader of his new ministry to tell him that the hug he had just given a girl had not been a complete side hug. My friend listened politely, then confidently yet respectfully explained to him that he had a very good gauge of his own personal struggles, and was spiritually mature enough to be able to know what things would be healthy for him or not. In response, the leader simply told him that he wasn't only worldly, he was also prideful.

Another friend, who was getting to know a girl he was interested in, was confronted by a youth leader about the relationship and told that it was unhealthy for him and that he needed to break it off. The two weren't dating, just simply talking to each other, and the leader took the student's phone and texted the girl himself to tell her that the student and she would no longer be talking to each other.

This student was twenty-one years old, the age some people are *getting married*, and he was being treated like a first grader, or someone unable to think and act for himself, just for *talking* to a girl he liked. The number of lines crossed by *taking his phone* and texting the girl *as him* is simply astounding and incredibly damaging to one's image and self-confidence.

The stories shared during these back-from-college gatherings were sickening. Instead of being filled with the joy of witnessing God in new and exciting places, almost every person came to that group each week exhausted, irritated, and even confused about the truth in these scenarios. They felt misunderstood, like they were one of the few in their ministries who were perceived as less spiritually mature.

They felt alone, as if to hold their ground where they felt God was calling them was to forfeit the acceptance of the people who were supposed to be there alongside them. In many scenarios, they came to our weekly group feeling shame, as over the course of months away at college, they had begun to believe that maybe they really were failing in their faith.

Most of all, they felt unheard. In nearly every account, these students had attempted to speak to a leader about what they were experiencing, hoping to start a dialogue and have their voices heard earnestly in an attempt to help change the unhealthy way things were being done. But in nearly every circumstance, they were written off, invalidated, minimized, or ignored altogether.

Interestingly enough, their woes weren't directed solely

towards these other ministries. One of my friends shared her trepidation coming *back* to our home church every break after being away at college. According to her, coming back to her home church was "like walking on eggshells," as it was always difficult for her to try and figure out what the new rules were since she had been away. And she wasn't alone.

These nights were supposed to end at nine, yet often ended up lasting hours longer, sometimes even until about one thirty in the morning, because of how thirsty everyone was to have their voices heard and their thoughts validated, as well as hear about the freeing effects the Holy Spirit can have on individual lives and whole ministries. A goal of these nights when my parents organized them was to encourage the college students and remind them of who they are to God. But they were utterly heartbroken by just how badly we all needed it.

Through the course of the summer, and week after week of meeting and hearing my friends' stories, another revelation was made abundantly clear to me. Every person has problems. And every church, composed of a bunch of people, definitely has problems. This is not abnormal and is not in itself grounds for serious authoritative reconstruction. The real harm comes when problems are noticed and communicated in the hopes of being resolved, but no attempts are made to change things.

From conversations with other members of our church, including both youth and adults, it became more apparent by the day that there were *way* more people aware of and experiencing these issues than just the younger demographic. Over the next several months, as the discourse surrounding the circumstances rose drastically, advances were made towards coming together as a church family and dissecting some of the issues that members had been noticing and experiencing. My mom was especially motivated to initiate discourse to help find solutions to these problems. What we didn't know was that these attempts had been made an innumerable amount of times over the years, each ending on practically the same note.

After talks with several church leaders, including our head pastor, the idea was agreed upon to create and send out an anonymous survey to the congregation, allowing them the opportunity to voice their concerns without fear of being made known. Initially, nobody really knew what kind of response to expect and how many of these surveys would be completed and sent back in. We all knew that people were experiencing these things, but there were still differing beliefs about how widespread and prevalent they were to the church body as a whole.

Then they started to come in.

Initially, only eighty surveys were sent to a portion of the congregation, and within only forty-eight hours, fifty-nine of them were returned, fully completed. It was simultaneously validating and heartbreaking seeing that the accounts shared in them were nearly identical across the board: stories of extreme rigidity between guys and girls; parents whose children were treated with immeasurable shame for things that nobody should ever experience shame for; and through all of them a deep, soul level hurt and pain caused by the severe spiritualistic legalism that had been coursing through our church like a disease overtaking a human nervous system for years and years.

It was a terrible thing hearing what our friends and peers had been going through, but there was also a sense of unified hope. Many people were scared, as in the past when they had voiced their thoughts and concerns, they had been shut down and invalidated. But now, with the sheer number of people speaking out in confidence, yet with love and grace, there was a silver lining on the horizon.

However, after those first forty-eight hours, the surveys stopped coming in. As it turned out, not all of the leaders were thrilled about the idea of church members having issues with the way things were being done.

Nobody expected such an overwhelming response from these surveys, and when it became clear just how pertinent the issues were, one of the leaders requested that no more surveys be allowed to be received or sent to the remainder of the congregation. It was disheartening to hear that the efforts toward change were being obstructed, but there was still an overwhelming response in those first two days.

Based on the mind-boggling response in such a short amount of time, it became clear to our head pastor that people needed to be heard more directly. Within twenty-four hours, a "town hall meeting" style gathering was organized by the pastor and my mom for the very next day after Sunday service, and an invite was sent out to the same recipients of the survey. Despite such short notice, when the time for the meeting arrived, the room was packed.

Though the meeting was scheduled to be ninety minutes, it lasted for nearly four hours as people took turns sharing their stories and voicing their concerns about the way they, or someone they knew, had been treated. It was shocking and eye-opening for many of the leaders present, and by the end, many people had a newfound hope that their voices were heard and that change might actually be on the horizon. Yet, as weeks went by, then months, the end result was simply... nothing. Nothing happened.

During the meeting, it had seemed that many of the church leaders, especially our head pastor, were keen on working to help make our church ecosystem healthier, yet after all was said and done, it felt as if no meeting had taken place at all. Acknowledgment of the accounts shared through the surveys and the meeting from the higher-ups in our church was virtually nonexistent. In the cases where the woes of church members *were* acknowledged, their feelings were often written off and deflected as being the result of their own individual problems rather than anything having to do with the church.

Now, I'm not saying it is solely the job of leaders to set change into motion. Absolutely not. In these scenarios, though, the church body had shown up, eager and willing to put effort into working together towards a solution. But a church can only succeed in such attempts if its leaders are by their side. And in this particular scenario, as it had been for decades, while some genuinely desired to help, many didn't and, in many cases, were even contesting our efforts to simply make our church a healthier place.

While people seemed, for the most part, to be "heard" by ministry leaders in the moment, there was no attempt to set the groundwork for any change whatsoever. In many cases, those most outspoken about their desires were ignored, minimized, and invalidated, as if those in leadership hoped that if no acknowledgment were given, eventually, the voices would die down, and people would give up.

The unfortunate reality is that sometimes, a church's true mission is not to lead people toward Christ, but rather to lead people into submission. Some church leaders don't want to give power to God, but hoard it for themselves. The members of a ministry may be led by voices of authority telling them that they are being brought closer to God, when in reality, many facets of their lives are actually catering to a starvation of spiritual freedom and lack of intimacy with Christ.

While many at some point come to the realization that this is happening, sadly, a good number never do, and instead buy into the hierarchy of legalistic church authority. We are becoming so lax in our spiritual lives that our loyalty to the church is becoming more important than our loyalty to God. After all, our standing in the church seemingly has a much more immediate and tangible effect on our daily lives, so why shouldn't it take precedence? We may be on "good terms" with God, but if we are in the way of our church's mission, we will be labeled as being against His will anyway.

It was during this time, after hearing the outcry of those around me, and seeing their voices met with closed eyes and turned heads, that I made the decision to leave my church. After twenty years, I was finally convinced that the problems that our church faced would not get better if it wasn't agreed upon by those in charge that anything was actually in need of changing. Some people wanted it this way, *needed* things to remain the same, or else risk losing some of the things they had decided were more important than God. And if a church places anything over God, it does not deserve to be called a church at all.

While my time at this church was at an end, the rest of my family did remain in the ministry for a while longer, attempting to navigate and encourage the push towards the change many desperately sought. The final straw for them came in the form of a conversation with another higher up in our church regarding my younger sister, who was in the children's ministry at that time.

My parents and this leader were discussing their issues with the extremely legalistic and shame-based structures by which the kid's ministry was being operated. The way it stood at the time, each child was required to study for and pass a "Bible test" in order to graduate to the next level class. Those who were able to memorize and recite their verses and successfully pass the other tenets of their exam-like evaluation were granted a ribbon, which would be seen by the rest of their class, while those who didn't would be seen as the ones in their class without one. These children were in elementary school and were already being taught that their spiritual value was derived not from their relationship with God but from how well they could perform on Bible-based memorization and theology evaluations.

Obviously, my parents had an issue with this, and spoke with this leader in an attempt to figure out a better method (which, to be honest, shouldn't be very hard to do, as there are *quite a few* better alternatives). However, rather than admit how unhealthy this system was, this leader simply told my parents that, since their daughter, my sister, was only in this ministry for a short amount of time every week, surely her time at home, along with the healthy teachings and guidance provided to her by my parents, would "balance it out."

My family was gone by the following Sunday.

Life in this church was the only life I had ever known. Up until those last several months, I had fully believed that I would be there until the day I died. I believed I would be married there. I would have a family there. I would watch my children grow up there and see them become Christ followers and eventually have families of their own. I would grow old there, surrounded by people who had been right beside me all those years.

That's the future that I had always seen. For my entire life, above all questions, doubts, and mysteries of what my future would entail, there was an assuredness that I would still be *there*, at my church, with the people who I had done life with since I was born and would continue to do life with until the very end. Yet, in a matter of months, that indestructible, infallible vision began to fade away, like a flame set to a leaf, slowly dissipating until it was nonexistent.

For the first time in my entire life, my vision for the future was unclear. I couldn't see it, because there was no foundation off which to base it. I had absolutely no idea what was next. And yet, though the uncertainty was daunting, I must admit, I imagined leaving would be more difficult than it actually was.

It was time. God had made it clear, through hurt and heartbreak and disappointment. Through pain and confusion and letdown. Yet, in the end, in confidence, clarity, and faith, it was clear that, though the future was uncertain, the present was in full view. What I had to do next, the very next step that I needed to take, was definite, and there was no ambiguity about it.

In the end, the most difficult part about leaving my church wasn't the actual act of leaving the ministry itself but the people I was leaving behind in it. The church was responsible for the majority of my deepest, longest-lasting relationships. But now, the question that confronted me was if the church was the only glue holding those relationships together, and whether those friendships would still have the roots to survive if taken out of the context in which they were constructed.

Sometimes, it can be hard to distinguish whether or not the people around you are friends out of intentionality or mere convenience. We have "friends" in many areas of our lives that are solely subjected to that one area. We have work friends, school friends, apartment building friends, sports team friends...the list goes on.

You are familiar with these people, maybe even pretty close. In some cases, you've known them for a long time, sometimes years and years. But when you graduate, or get a different job, or move to a new home, all of a sudden... you never see them again. At first you didn't think much of it. But at some point it occurs to you that those friends you had made hadn't been the real, deep friendships that stick with you for the rest of your life. They had only been "phase friendships," friendships made at a particular phase of our lives that dissipate as we move on.

I assumed many of my friendships at church weren't phase friendships. I *hoped* they weren't. Yet, I was still fearful. What if I lost contact with my close friends? We definitely won't see each other as often. What if some of my friends stop talking to me *because* of my decision to leave our church?

I had some friends I doubted would let such a decision affect our relationship, yet others I wasn't so sure of. But I was sure of one thing. If the friends I have are real friends, they still will be even after I leave. Because real friendships aren't confined to the four walls of a church, or a school, or an office. Our real friends will stick by our side, even when we venture out of the familiar and into the unknown. I knew that the friends worth keeping wouldn't fade away once I left.

And I'm grateful to say that they didn't.

PART IV

ALL THAT REMAINS

14

A JUMBLE OF CRUMPLED PAPERS

Imagine with me for a moment, all of the thoughts and ideas currently in your brain. Thousands. Tens of thousands. *Hundreds* of thousands. Millions? I'm not sure exactly what kind of numbers we're dealing with when thinking about all of the thoughts that our mind stores.

Simply put, it's incredible—a masterwork of design and ingenuity. The very framework for how we view and experience the world around us is composed of all the thoughts we have about it all. In a sense, who we are directly results from the cumulation of all those thoughts, ideas, and beliefs. And as we go through life, the changing and development of those thoughts and ideas also changes us.

What happens in our brain when a new idea is added to the mix? You learn a new word, memorize a new song, or maybe take on a whole new language. You make a mistake, and learn what went wrong for next time. You have a positive or negative experience with someone, and based on that interaction, gain new views on what kind of person they are. Every experience, every situation, every moment, the world around us influences the thoughts and ideas we construct, which then in turn influences how we see the world.

When thinking about this process of the brain forging a new idea, the visual that comes to my mind is a desk in a dimly lit room, its wooden surface illuminated by the tungsten glow of a single lamp. In the middle of that desk is a single blank slip of paper, next to it a stack of additional blank slips of paper ascending towards the ceiling. There is a man sitting at that desk, or a woman, if you prefer, a pen in their grasp, hand poised over the blank page.

This person is our mind incarnate, or maybe our consciousness. Every time a new idea is formed, the pen in their hand drops to the page at lightning speed, scribbling so fast dust clouds appear around the paper like an animated cartoon. The idea is cemented in writing, and the slip of paper is fit into one of those plastic cylinders that you see at drive through banks. Mr. (or Mrs.) Mind then lifts the cylinder up to the suction tube above, and just like the scene from *Elf*, the idea is sucked up and away into the deep recesses of the brain, where it takes up a permanent residency and role in shaping and affecting us and our view of existence.

Assuming this is in fact the way in which new ideas are recorded (I have yet to be presented with any proof of the contrary), imagine just how many slips of paper there are in our minds. Cities composed entirely of towers of papers, all labeled and organized by different topics and categories pertaining to our individual lives.

There are all of your thoughts about Italian food. Indeed, garlic bread is a ten out of ten appetizer. In that stack over there is a box containing every view you have on math. Curiously, they're all pretty detailed until about Algebra 2, then the ink on the pages begins to fade. A ways down is an entire city block dedicated to your past, some streets lit with warm street lamps and cheerful string lights, as well as the occasional dark alleyway. The roads are lined with skyscrapers made entirely of tiny slips of paper, each tower pertaining to a specific year of your life.

So many slips of paper. So many thoughts, ideas, opinions, beliefs, fears, and dreams. All of them together forming who you are.

We don't become who we are overnight. Sure, we're always *somebody* at any given point in time, but to become who we were destined to be takes a while, the accumulation of slips of paper slowly molding and shaping us into the people we are now, and the people we will become in the future. We are never stagnant in our development as people. We are always changing, often by tiny, barely noticeable steps, or slips of paper, at a time. All of the beliefs in our minds are continuously altering and evolving. As we grow older and go through life, experiencing all kinds of situations, we come out the other side having obtained new ideas and insights.

When we are young, the beliefs we obtain are often taken on for the first time, filling a space in our subconscious where no preexisting idea dwelled before. But what happens when we are exposed to a new idea or belief that *contradicts* something we already believe?

Say you have never before had ice cream (I know, I'm going *really* dark here). If you have never tried ice cream and see an advertisement saying that Rocky Road is the best flavor ever to exist, with your limited, or in this case nonexistent firsthand knowledge, you might take on that belief. You don't know for sure, but if someone else is saying it, there's a good chance it could be true. The belief is written on a slip of paper and added to the library in your mind.

But then, the glorious day comes when you find yourself at an ice cream shop. You ask for a sample of Rocky Road, and it's not bad, but then you taste Cookies 'N Cream and realize that what you believed was far from true. Cookies 'N Cream is undoubtedly the reigning king of ice cream flavors, and Rocky Road pales in comparison. When the idea that Rocky Road is the best flavor was initially added to your brain, there was no original idea to pit it against. But now that you believe something different, this new idea about Cookies 'N Cream must *replace* the idea about Rocky Road.

Obviously, in this made-up scenario, this person has only ever tried two flavors of ice cream, so that idea may be contested again in the future. (But let's be honest. Nothing beats Cookies 'N Cream, so I don't see it happening anytime soon). Additionally, this person's belief about ice cream flavors is not a fact by any means, but simply their own opinion. Regardless, they have now had to reevaluate what they *initially* believed with the new information they have been given to decide what they *now* believe to be true. They've lived a little longer, experienced a little more, and have decided that their perspective has changed.

This is a good thing, as the longer we go through life, and the more of our beliefs are challenged and refined, the closer we come to really figuring out who we truly are, and what we truly believe. But the process of re-evaluating our beliefs isn't always as easy and painless as figuring out our favorite ice cream flavor. Oftentimes, both *realizing* that an idea is no longer what we believe and having to *replace* it can result in a very rocky and uncertain period of time while we take an introspective look at what these changes mean for how we define ourselves and the world around us. A very rocky road indeed.

Everybody experiences these periods of re-evaluation in their lives, moments where we have to pit what we have previously believed about something up to that point with what we now realize we believe more. Based on the way we now see something works, our old understanding just doesn't cut it anymore, and we must take the steps to replace those old mentalities with the new.

While this happens on a smaller, relatively harmless scale pretty much every day, there are also many cases where these seasons of re-evaluation are born out of difficult and painful circumstances. However, no matter the context, they always have the potential to result in positive change.

Upon leaving the church I had grown up in, I found myself smack dab in the middle of such a season. For twenty years, I had been a spiritual sponge, soaking up all of the beliefs, teachings, practices, and viewpoints presented to and sometimes imposed upon me by those in my spiritual community. When I was younger, most of the simple, foundational teachings I was given were grounded in truth. But as I grew older and those teachings evolved, many of them grew into unhealthy, even destructive ideologies that, in the end, resulted in me finding myself at a crossroads of where I belonged and what I believed.

I had spent my entire life up to that point filling my head with slips of paper of all the beliefs and ideas I had about God, church, and spirituality, ranging from the simplest foundational principles to more intricate and debatable notions. For example:

God is real.

Jesus died so that I could be forgiven of all of my sins.

*Christianity is the truest religion and the only way to get to
Heaven.*

Everything in Scripture is God-breathed and 100% accurate.

*The way The Church does things is exactly how God desires them
to be done.*

The list goes on. I believed each and every idea so
deeply, so indisputably, as they were some of the strongest
foundational pillars of who I knew myself to be. And, up
until this point, they had never been challenged to a degree
in which I felt any reason to question them.

But my once indestructible belief system started
showing cracks as I began to realize what I once thought to
be impossible: that among the many truths that my faith
comprised, there were also falsities, which had infiltrated
what I had thought to be an impenetrable shield of faith. I
experienced betrayal, dishonesty, shame, duplicity, and arti-
ficiality, all in the name of God. And the more aware I
became of these things, the more I realized that they hadn't
suddenly come out of nowhere. They had been going on my
whole life, and well before I was born.

The backbone for a vast majority of my Christian beliefs
was my faith in the church itself. So, naturally, as that faith
began to waver and eventually diminish, most of these other
sentiments also began to be called into question. "I'm not
sure the Church is always seeking God's will. What does
that say about the God they claim to follow? Or the Bible
they claim to live by? Or the rules that they say Christians
are supposed to adhere to? Is the Bible completely God-
breathed? Is the Bible inspired by God *at all?* What if Christianity isn't the only way to Heaven? What if Christianity
was completely made up by people whose only desire was

to use religion as a tool to gain power, control, and money? What if Jesus was just a figure we made up to validate our desire to be forgiven for all the bad things we do? Does Jesus, or God, or Heaven actually exist, or is it all the fabricated result of humanity's soul-crushing inability to comprehend death?"

The questions begin small. They always do. In my own experience, the simple doubt in how my church operated led me down a long tunnel of questions and apprehension toward my faith as a whole, eventually cascading into some very big, very real questions. What were once my most steadfast convictions were suddenly the object of most scrutiny and debate. I now realized that I could no longer be *absolutely sure* which things I believed were true and which were not.

With this one simple admission, the wall protecting the paper city in my mind began to crumble, allowing the wind to come rushing in; a violent, chaotic gust that tore unforgivingly through the streets, sending every idea about God and church I had accumulated over my entire life into the air in a whirlwind of confusion.

Instead of slips of paper pristinely stacked in piles and organized into boxes, the stacks were toppling, papers strewn, ripped, and mashed together, until what remained was a giant jumble of crumpled papers, a cacophony of incoherent noise that seemed impossible to distinguish. I had attained twenty years' worth of ideologies, principles, and ways of thinking that I had grown up believing wholeheartedly. And because so many were originally founded on biblical truths, on some level and to some degree, it seemed like an overwhelming and nearly impossible task to differentiate those truths from the spiritual inaccuracies and distortions that had been blended into them.

But I wasn't simply going to throw out everything I

knew and believed. Deep down, I *knew* that many of my beliefs were still valid. Just because some of them were stained with false principles and damaging ideologies did not mean that they were untrue at their purest roots. But in order to figure out for myself which ideas I still believed and which I didn't, I had some work to do.

There was a jumble of crumpled papers in my mind, comprising every belief and idea I had ever had about God, church, religion, faith, even myself, and I was determined to differentiate those I deemed true from those I now knew were false. I was faced with the task of removing the slips of paper from this massive entanglement one by one, smoothing them out, and under great discernment, holding them up to the light to see if they still fit in the context of what I knew to be true about God.

If the answer was yes, I would place them in a new pile. If not, they would be discarded, tossed in the trash, and replaced with a refined idea that I was now confident was centered in God.

* * *

A few years back, my family had to have our house fumigated due to termites. To get rid of them, a tent was wrapped around the entire house and sealed tight. Then, a pesticide gas was released to kill every last one of them. You've probably seen a house in this process at some point, most likely while driving down the street. You can't miss it. It usually looks like a circus.

In a way, this process of reassessment was like a personal and spiritual fumigation. My home was being infested by an unwanted entity, which was a negligence to Christ where Christ should be most present. Obviously, when you get pests in your home, you don't want to abandon it. Your home isn't the problem; it's what is invading it. I knew there was truth in Christianity, that I belonged there, but I needed to flush out the parts that I knew didn't belong. If I didn't, who knows how long it would be until the whole house was overrun?

It's a daunting and taxing task, both in terms of time and emotional energy, to sift through every single idea and belief you may have at one point believed wholeheartedly, perhaps even blindly. And while there is certainly a starting point, I don't think it ever really ends. It's a continual process of assessment and discernment of what you believe in contrast (or unison) with what is being presented to you.

As I write this, I am still doing it, as day by day, certain situations and interactions will bring a particular idea into question, often one that I hadn't thought about for a long time, which I will then have to really think about to determine if there is still a place for it in my constantly evolving and developing view of God. And slowly, one idea at a time, that jumble of crumpled papers gets smaller and smaller, the noise returns to a normal frequency, and the assurance in every one of my beliefs grows stronger and stronger.

But sadly, for so many people in similar positions, this is the place that marks the end of their relationship with God. They have spent precious time of their lives, many of them years, holding the notion that there must be something more to life than what so many settle for. They find the Church, where they sow in the hope of achieving something deeper, but in the end are left thrown out on the curb in the rain, holding their jumble of crumpled papers in their hands, all of the beliefs and ideas that for so long defined not only how they saw the world and God, but also how they saw themselves.

At that point, many people look down at those crumpled papers and see this way of life as yet another empty promise that they had clung to, hoping it would be real, that resulted in useless ideas that only ended up hurting them and leading them down a path they never wanted to go. So they dump that jumble of crumpled papers on the ground or a nearby dumpster, discarding every idea and belief about God and Christianity, and move on with their life, leaving any ties to God behind them for good.

But it doesn't have to be this way. Because the truths and promises of God are real, and they can change your life if you can find them in their fullest, truest forms.

While God will take us where we're at, no matter how certain we are, the better we understand these truths and promises that He gives us, the deeper and fuller our relationship with Him can be. When finding myself at this same crossroads, I am grateful that I had been given a deep enough knowledge and understanding to know that those things that didn't seem like God really weren't. And because of that, I was able to see that God in His true form was in fact there for me to discover.

I was tired and exasperated with the ways in which God was being presented, how His love and promises were being warped and misconstrued in ways that manipulated and hurt people, including myself. And in the end, many people's faith was blind, not due to a complete trust in God, but because they had been conditioned not to question what they were being taught.

So when the time came for me to finally begin sifting through my jumble of crumpled papers, I had a contingency. While I was deconstructing the faith I had accrued, I did not want to reconstruct a faith of the same nature. I wanted this new faith to be rebuilt in accordance with reason, rather than in compromise of it.

Everything that we believe about God that is true can be pitted against reason without faltering. Yet we are so afraid that if pondered for too long or thought about too deeply, the holes will start to show, and those biblical truths will prove failing. Now I know that should these ideas and beliefs fail in the face of reason, it only means that the idea was not one hundred percent of God. Maybe fifty percent. Maybe more. But not completely.

The Holy Spirit leads us to all truth, and if a concept about God is completely true and how God desires us to know it, the Spirit will validate it in our hearts through the supporting evidence of reason. Yes, there are aspects of God that *transcend* reason, questions left by the absolute magnitude of His being that reason cannot answer. However, there is no part of God that *defies* reason. As such, when introduced to the equation of God, reason will always endorse, and never contradict His testaments.

Maybe you have your own jumble of crumpled papers. Most people do, and it doesn't only pertain to their perspective on God. There are so many areas of life that we give ourselves to, only to later learn that the ideas associated with them were nowhere near what we have now grown to believe. Many people don't deal with it. Because they can't, or at least they don't believe they have the ability to. Especially if they know enough to know that their beliefs aren't entirely accurate, yet still lack a thorough enough understanding to know what the truth actually is. That is perhaps the scariest place to be, and the place where most people decide to call it quits out of fear of what they don't know.

> **Untruth:** *It Is Dangerous to Re-Evaluate Your Beliefs*
> **Truth:** *It Is Essential To Re-Evaluate Your Beliefs In Order to Attain Deeper Convictions*

15

SLEEPING IN ON A SUNDAY

I remember the first Sunday I didn't go to church. Technically, there was a smattering of one-offs throughout the years where my Sunday mornings weren't spent in a congregation, but this was the first time that it was because I no longer considered myself a member.

You might think I spent that morning glancing at the clock, wondering what songs the worship team had chosen to play that day, what jokes the pastor was cracking on stage, or perhaps who noticed my absence. But to be honest, I wasn't thinking about any of those things during the time service was taking place.

Because I was asleep.

My first impression of a churchless Sunday morning was how refreshing it was to wake up fully rested.

I did have those thoughts once I woke up, however. Most can probably relate to the sentiment that church isn't solely a two-hour commitment on Sunday mornings. More times than not, it's a full-day affair.

Growing up, a typical Sunday would usually start with the main service. If you were on the serving team or had some type of discussion group beforehand, you would show up an hour or two early. After service, the socialites would stick around to catch up with friends, seemingly competing to see who could be the last person remaining in the courtyard. Post-church lunch is a must and is often spent with church friends. My family hosted a small group at our house for a few years, and the families who came would pick up lunch on the way over. The actual group would last a good hour or so, but the house wasn't empty of guests for double or triple that time.

During holiday breaks and three-day weekends, I usually had friends come home with us after service, and we would spend the rest of the day in the guest house, which my family had converted into a DIY movie theater, where we would play video games and watch movies while simultaneously having hours-long conversations about whatever was prevalent in our lives at that particular point in time.

We may not have been singing worship songs. We may not have been reading scripture. But in a very real way, it was church. It was connection. It was communion. It was people enjoying each other's company and venturing through life together. Whether we were eating pizza, cracking jokes, and slaying zombies until the sun came up or sharing in each other's hurt and heartache for just as long, there in that back room, we were experiencing church. Perhaps in its rawest form. Even when we didn't know it.

For me, church didn't just take place on Sunday at eleven. It was an ongoing experience, not simply attended, but lived alongside the people going through life with you. That first Sunday, missing service wasn't the thing that occupied my thoughts the most. It was the rest of the church experience that would most likely never be the same ever again. I remember that Sunday being a very long day because of how much time there was to spend doing nothing. And it was quiet.

It never felt like I had made the wrong decision. If anything, I was constantly reaffirmed that I had done what I had been meant to do. But moving on is always hard, as with such a decision comes an awareness that, alongside the things you may be relieved to leave behind, there are also some things that you wish you didn't have to. Some things that, if you could, you would hold on to forever. Even when you're moving on to something better, you mourn the loss of the things that were truly good.

For the first time in my life, I found myself separated from what I had grown to believe was the routine Christian lifestyle. I wasn't going to church. I didn't have a small group. I was still in college and wasn't a part of a campus ministry. For the first time since the day I was born, I was no longer in the heart of it all. Instead of being smack dab in the center of all of the commotion of Christianity, I was an onlooker, peering in from the outside. And it was there, on the outskirts, where I found myself afforded the freedom, for what felt like the first time, to discern, contemplate and wrestle with any idea I wanted without the expectation or pressure to view or perceive it in a prescribed way.

I was still a Christian. As if that needed to be said. If anything, everything I was doing was in an effort to *preserve* my faith, not because I was deciding to turn away from it. I desired a deeper faith. A *truer* faith. And it was clear to me that in order to gain such a faith, I had to step out into deeper waters. I had to allow myself to wrestle with ideas and doubts that I had been taught would be a risk to my relationship with God if entertained. After striving my whole adolescent life to achieve and maintain an undisputed certainty in everything I believed, I had to honestly admit that there were things I was uncertain about.

If I truly wanted a more authentic faith, I had to venture beyond the boundary lines of "safe spirituality" and view my uncertainties not as weak points in my faith but as stepping stones toward real, satisfying answers, fully accepting that in some cases, the conclusions I might end up coming to may not always lead to the "religiously correct" resolutions. By now I knew that it was not religion I was after. In many cases, it was what I least desired. What I wanted was truth. I wanted God. I wanted Christ. And the more questions I allowed myself to confront with no preconceived notions or spiritual bias, the greater possibility I would have of landing closest to the truth.

I was entering an entirely new phase of my life, leaving much of the familiar behind and walking into a world of unknowns. I had my jumble of crumpled papers, which I was working through day by day, moment by moment, one idea at a time. I was asking questions, more than I ever had before, about things that I would never have assumed I would ever be questioning. Things that for so many years had seemed obvious, steadfast, and absolute. I was curious, yet also scared, about what I might find. But I was hopeful, knowing that this was undoubtedly the best opportunity I had ever been given to figure out what I believed.

The Bible tells us we cannot serve two masters, and for most of my life I had been unwittingly disobeying this instruction. While I believed I was serving God alone, I was really serving God and the Church as separate entities, convinced that they were one and the same. But now, I had released those bonds, and only had to listen to a single voice, which I knew would lead me exactly where I needed to go.

But it wasn't going to be a smooth ride, as if up until this point it had been anything of the sort. I was skirting the far edges of faith, wrestling with concepts I had very little experience dealing with; ideas that are often looked at unfavorably and pushed as far away from the spotlight of spiritual focus as possible. And while the freedom was undeniably invigorating, with it came some less than satisfactory attributes.

What I quickly realized was that in order to be able to fully gain an understanding of the role that these ideas played in my life, I had to first resolve the turmoil they were causing inside of me.

16

SEEKING THE UNCERTAINTY

I gotta be honest. I don't have many regrets in my life.

There are things I could have done differently, or better, or maybe avoided altogether. Things that caused hurt and pain to myself and others. But there are very few things I would actually change about my past if I could go back and do it over. I believe that everything that happens happens for a reason, and both the good and bad things play an equal role in our development into the people we become and our view of God. However, there is one thing that I can whole-heartedly say I regret from the first twenty years of my life.

I regret how little I doubted.

I never once doubted the existence of God. Since the day I learned how to walk, I was taught that He was always the one guiding each of my steps. He gifted every skill or talent I possessed in the hopes that I would utilize them for His glory. The sun was an expression of His joy, the clouds and rain His grief. Every breath I breathed was granted to me solely out of an act of grace, and with such breath came the charge to pronounce His goodness and love to any hearing ear.

And when a light fixture comes crashing to the floor exactly where you stood only seconds before, there is no other explanation than the intervention of the divine.

These are the things I was told from my very earliest memories. And thank God (literally) that they were. While many children are raised in broken homes, some with abusive, neglectful, or simply distant parents, being taught that they are alone and the meaning of their life is illusory, I was given ideas not of dejection and seclusion but of hope and solidarity.

I was constantly reminded not of life's meaninglessness, but of the meaning laced in every minute detail of our lives, sown into every thread of our being. Because of my upbringing, humanity wasn't simply living on a giant rock floating endlessly in space. Every person was brought into existence with direct intention, not to be slaves, outcasts, or wanderers, but to know our Creator and live in the wholeness that comes from His untamable love.

My gratitude for being born into a context where I was taught these things is immeasurable, as I genuinely believe in the core of my being that these foundational ideas about the God of the universe are the unequivocal truth. Yet, I can't help but find it slightly disconcerting how I never once expressed even the slightest amount of uncertainty in these things for the first twenty years of my life. Not merely the idea of God, who the thought of alone should invoke some questioning, but the concept of Jesus, who not only was the Son of God, born of a virgin through the power of the Holy Spirit, who was both fully God and fully man, but also performed a multitude of supernatural miracles, healed the sick just by touching them, told the future, walked on water, and rose from the dead.

Growing up in a religious environment, there is a "kid-friendly" version of the Bible and its message that inadvertently glosses over the fact that the majority of the things being described are completely and utterly abnormal and extraordinary (emphasis on "extra-ordinary"). Just as with those foundational ideas of God, I grew up being told all of these things about Jesus, the stories of His life narrated over and over with the casualness of an Aesop's fable.

I grew up believing that Jesus healed a man with leprosy simply by touching him with as much certainty as I knew my favorite color was blue. I knew He was born of a virgin before I even knew what sex was! And because of that, the sheer magnitude of these miraculous acts was reduced to much more mundane, everyday pieces of information.

It was still remarkable, and I knew that these things that happened in the Bible didn't happen every day. But instead of being something immense and challenging to grasp, it was common knowledge, simply because it was the only truth ever presented. There was no one around me questioning the validity of what we believed, or even suggesting that it took any amount of faith to believe it at all, so that's exactly how it was accepted.

I never doubted the truths of the Bible, not necessarily because I had *chosen* it as the most trustworthy information, but because it was presented as the only information that had any truth. It was never scrutinized under a microscope to ascertain its validity but instead was instilled in us as a basic understanding. We were learning that Jesus fed over five thousand people with five loaves of bread and two fish at the same time we were learning that Earth is the third planet from the Sun.

We believed these things not because we had dug into the material, wrestled with the ideas, and decided it was what we truly believed. It was what we were told was the unarguable truth, and we were afforded no room to question it.

Not that we would have if we were given the chance. At the ages we were, we had such robust and blind faith in not only the information being given to us, but the people giving it. I had grown up believing that every single thing the church had ever told me was one hundred percent correct. With that kind of track record, it only made sense that I trusted their discernment and guidance completely. So, naturally, as the "indisputable truths" being presented began to expand in scope, encompassing ideas pertaining to the authority of the church and its leaders and how I should conduct my own life, I still didn't question it.

Funnily enough, I think it was this exact trait, this unequivocal acceptance and confidence in every spiritual idea that was given to me, that contributed to my perception as such a "steadfast" Christian throughout my childhood and early teens.

I was often looked at extremely complimentarily among the leaders and others in my ministry as someone on the "right path." I was always the one showing up, always offering my time and energy, and always following the rules. I was someone whom nobody needed to keep an eye on because they were confident that I was always going to be exactly where they thought I needed to be.

It took over two decades for it to even cross my mind that perhaps our indisputable truths and principles could perhaps be disputed, and that many facets of our cause might in fact be fruitless. I don't blame my ignorance or naïveté. It was what I was born into. It is incredible how pivotal the context of our upbringing is in forming our perception of the world. If someone were to ask me, "Why are you a Christian?" I would have two answers which I believe are equally true:

One, I am a Christian because I believe that God exists, that He sent Jesus to live among us, who died for our sins and was resurrected, granting us freedom from the debt that those sins accrued.

And two, I am a Christian because my parents are.

Neither of these reasons for my faith is any less true than the other. My convictions about the truths of the Bible are just as responsible for my faith as the fact that I grew up knowing nothing else. If I had been born into a home that was not Christian, there is always the possibility that I would have found my faith along the way. Many do. But it is also entirely plausible, as is the case for hundreds of millions of people around the world, that I would never have been exposed to the Word of God, let alone the people to show me the power and truth it holds.

I will never know how God decides who is born where and into what circumstances. I believe that level of security clearance is reserved for those who live outside of time.

While some grow up in poverty, others are born into royalty. While one child is born to an abusive single father, another is raised by two loving, nurturing, and happily married parents. While someone across the world is brought up in a religion of hatred and violence, or perhaps no religion at all, I somehow found myself lucky enough to have been taught about Jesus. There may be a lot of crap that has been erected around Him, but by Himself, I believe that Jesus truly is the answer to life, and life to the fullest.

I, as well as many of my friends who were born into the church alongside me, considered ourselves Christians simply because we were raised by Christian parents and were taught that it was right. It wasn't that we didn't believe it was true, but it also wasn't because we had really done any of the hard, soul-searching work to come to that conclusion. In many ways, it had already been done for us. Which, really, is quite a remarkable thing. Our parents were the ones who truly "found" Jesus. Unlike us, they didn't grow up having Jesus served to them on a silver platter. They had to search for Him. And now that they knew Him, we could reap the benefits right off the bat.

Perhaps it is this very fact, that many of my peers and I never had to *search* for Jesus, that blurred the lines and understated the stark realities and extravagance that a relationship with Him provided us. Jesus had always been there, from my very earliest memories. He was never someone I had to live without. He was never somebody I didn't know, at least in a formal sense. There was no transition from a life without Him to a life with Him, and as such there was never a comparison of the integrity of the two.

All many of us had ever known was a life *with* Jesus. He wasn't our chosen life. He was our default. And though many of us did *choose* Him intentionally as we got older, while we were young, the Christian lifestyle was just a part of the package deal that came with being alive. All the beliefs, ideas, and "truths" that came with that lifestyle were the basis for everything we did and every way we thought.

* * *

It's no wonder I never doubted any of the ways things were done, and why it is especially hard for young people all over the world, especially those born into a particular religious environment, to be able to differentiate between good, healthy cultures and ideologies and false, harmful ones. From a very young age, these ideas are ingrained into us as being one hundred percent true and, in many cases, the only way to a full, satisfying, and even eternal life.

Additionally, in many spiritual communities, it is also cautioned that the doubting or rejection of any idea presented could spell disaster for the unfortunate person that finds themselves doing so. To doubt or challenge the principles laid out as the answers to life itself could only mean that you have been misled, confused, and may even be a danger to those around you by spreading such uncertainty like a virus. I didn't want that. My friends didn't want that. Who would? To doubt was to fail, and nobody wants to fail.

Doubt was a concept rarely approached in my church, and is treated the same in multitudes of churches around the world, as there is a fear that to question or have uncertainty toward any aspect of the doctrine taught means that one's faith is failing. One of the biggest lies about faith is that it is the absence of doubt. Yet this is how it is portrayed and viewed by so many.

Leagues of Christians are judging the depth and earnestness of their faith by how often or how seldom they doubt the Bible, God, or any aspect of Christianity, when in reality, these doubts and questions are often the very things that can lead to a deeper, more authentic faith.

I was recently reading atheist turned Christian Lee Strobel's book *The Case for Faith*, a follow-up to the widely known and praised *The Case for Christ*, in which he approaches theological experts with some of the hardest-hitting objections to the validity of Jesus, the Bible, and faith. One of the topics covered was the misconceptions about doubt in the lives of believers. At the start of each chapter, Strobel includes two quotes on the subject, one from an atheist and one from a Christian. I found both pertaining to doubt intriguing and highly pertinent:

> "In their most inner thoughts, even the most devout Christians know that there is something illegitimate about belief. Underneath their profession of faith is a sleeping giant of doubt... In my experience, the best way to conquer doubt is to yield to it." - Dan Baker, pastor-turned-atheist

"Those who believe they believe in God but without passion in the heart, without anguish of mind, without uncertainty, without doubt, and even at times without despair, believe only in the idea of God, and not in God himself." - Madeleine L'Engle, Christian author

Clearly, these are two distinctly opposing views on the idea of doubt, as while one claims that doubt is the proof that our faith in God is a fallacy, the other protests that our faith is a fallacy without it. Yet a drawing point that both viewpoints derive from and that I agree with completely is that most Christians will do anything in their power to keep their doubt buried under the facade of a bulletproof faith, as if such ideas are complete opposites.

There are so many questions, so many what ifs, and so many unquantifiable variables in our relationship with God that I would pose that there is no possible way to achieve a completely authentic faith without, at times, finding your-self in places of doubt. Yet, despite its central role in our spiritual lives, we act as if only the weakest of us experience it.

We have left little room for doubt in Contemporary Christian Culture (You didn't think I forgot about the magnificent CCC, did you?). We have been sold the lie that to doubt the legitimacy of God, or any aspect of our spiri-tual lives for that matter, is to prove that we have failed to gain an authentic, grounded, and infallible faith.

Sadder still, those who are in the midst of choosing to follow God allow that lie to determine for them the fact that due to their unresolved doubts, they are not deserving of such a faith, and many become dispirited and decide God may not actually be for them because of their own short-comings. After all, with so much inauthentic Christianity proclaiming the necessity for unquestioning faith, there would surely be no place for doubt. To quote Os Guinness, also included in *The Case for Faith*, "The shame is not that people have doubts, but that they are ashamed of them."

During the process of re-evaluating my faith, piecing together my beliefs, and scrapping the harmful ideologies and practices from the past, not only was there confusion in having to decipher the good from the bad, but there was also hurt, pain, and wounds that inevitably resulted in doubts spanning nearly every corner of the Christian ethos. Naturally, I had reservations about the church, including not only its institutions and viewpoints but also its members. Questions such as "Do people who go to church actually want God, or do they just seek to follow spiritual authority, no matter what form it takes?"

But my thoughts didn't end with church. Due to how deeply intertwined church and God were in my life growing up, I felt the negative aspects of my experience seeping into my resolve about God as a whole.

I knew what I believed about God. For every unhealthy thing I took on growing up, I also gained real, authentic insight and knowledge about God. I had those foundational truths, even if many of them were not fully developed or learned to their fullest extent. Yet once I was in a position where my trust had been betrayed by those who had been the teachers of that knowledge and understanding through the years, and that once completely dependable rock on which my belief was founded began showing cracks, I didn't know where the truth stopped and the falsities began. Everything had been undeniably true until, all at once, it wasn't.

Despite knowing what I knew, I was suddenly unsure if any of it was correct at all. And because of this, I sat in a prolonged period of uncertainty with even some of the most basic principles of the Christian faith. Are Christian teachings reliable at all? What if the Bible is completely made up? Is God even real? What if this is all some agenda-motivated attempt at converting people into submission?

Some of these thoughts, especially the most fundamental ones, didn't last very long. I knew God was real. If I ever had any doubt about that, I would look out the window and think about the complex intricacies of the world, nature, and humans, and I would have no question that it was all intentionally created. Yet that didn't mean that they still didn't cross my mind, usually when I thought through specific situations growing up or heard of some other well-known church leader or ministry being convicted of abuse, corruption, or fraud.

In today's world, there is so much noise from all sides that you can put together a convincing argument for or against practically anything, with viable evidence and reasoning. I had been going to church since I was born and had at this point been baptized for over five years. In all that time, I had never doubted such central aspects of my faith. But now, all of a sudden, I was finally entertaining the possibility that everything I knew, and I mean *everything*, could potentially be wrong. For the first time, I needed more than the assurances of the people around me. I needed to seek the answers and come to those conclusions myself.

People have doubts for a plethora of reasons. They can come from places of hurt, such as personal or family wounds. They can come from false beliefs and, therefore, disillusions and disappointments with God. Even different seasons of life can lead people to uncertainties about various aspects of the things they believe or ways they live.

Whatever the reason for your doubt, one thing is undeniably certain. Doubt is not the opposite of faith. A healthy faith is never stagnant. It is continually growing, always evolving, and the measure of such growth is by recognizing the areas of doubt and uncertainty and seeking to satisfy the question marks. The man who came to Jesus with his demon-possessed son in the book of Mark summarizes this dynamic perfectly in a single sentence when he tells Jesus, "I believe. Help me overcome my unbelief!"

Faith is not all-encompassing, meaning we don't believe all or nothing. All of us are somewhere on the spectrum, knowing what we know and believing what we believe, but always learning more and confronting new challenges in what, and who, we place our faith in. This man talking with Jesus knew this well and was secure enough in that fact to know that the very best thing he could possibly do was not to try to hide his uncertainties, but profess them to Jesus, pleading with Him to lead him to the answers.

How rich this relationship can be, with us accepting and admitting where our faith falters and going to Jesus to help guide us further. This is how God designed it, yet because of false standards and ideologies of perfection, we are embarrassed by our doubts, perceiving them as weaknesses. But we fail to realize that they are not failures, but opportunities to seek God, who promises that if we do so with our whole heart, we will in fact find what we are after.

We fear that if we are honest about our doubts, others will think we are weak in our faith, and because we believe there's a chance they could be right, we lock up our doubts somewhere deep in our hearts.

In many cases, Christians deny the existence of any doubt and live by a blind faith that is so deaf to the voice of their hearts and minds that it fails to actually be of any substance. It is too shallow to offer any power because we have not nurtured it by allowing Jesus to feed and validate His truths in our souls. This is where such a fantastically dismal amount of believers live their entire lives, settling for a faith that is in complete deprivation of any actual friction.

And if there is no friction in your faith, no substantial obstacle in which your faith is needed to overcome, is it really faith at all?

> **Untruth**: *Doubt Is A Sign of Weak Faith*
> **Truth**: *The Lack of Doubt Is A Sign of Stagnant Faith*

Heed your doubts. Understand the questions you have, the blank spaces you desire to be filled, with the knowledge that they can indeed be filled should you seek the answers. If you believe that God is who He says He is and has the ability to do everything He promises, then you can be confident that every doubt you have, no matter how colossal or demanding, can be satisfied to its utmost extent.

That is not to say that every question will be answered in its most direct form. If we were granted the absolute knowledge of every single thing we sought, we wouldn't need faith. But answers will be given where they are assured, and where they are not, your faith will be elevated to satisfy the longing that comes with the unknown.

17

CYNICS AND SPONGES

I have a confession to make.

I'm a cynic.
And the odds are, you are too.
Is it healthy?
No.
Is it who God wants us to be?
Nada.

Yet, at some point or another, every one of us has experienced having a cynical perspective of something or someone.

In fact, many of us have something *right now* that we are cynical of as a result of a past hurt, pain, or abuse of trust or power. I am fully aware of my cynical attitude towards various aspects of Christianity due to what I have experienced over the years. Yet, at the same time, I've reached a point where I can distinguish my cynicism from what I know is the truth.

Cynicism isn't always wrong or inaccurate. That's

honestly what can make it so hard to shake. It's not always as easy as telling yourself that your negative thoughts are not true. Sometimes they are. *Oftentimes* they are. A concept I've heard is that cynicism is truth, but without God.

Have you ever tried arguing with a cynic? How'd that go for you? If I could take a guess, I would say not great. The problem when trying to convince a cynic who doesn't add God to the equation of their circumstances is that you will usually never get anywhere. You will almost always be proven wrong because, for the most part, they're usually correct in accurately discerning the truth of the world and the humans in it.

I think we can all agree that people are pretty messed up. We do bad things—*all* the time. And without God to show us how we can become a little less messed up, there really isn't much hope for the negative aspects of our lives, ourselves, and other people.

Without God, cynicism becomes your truth; usually, no one will be able to "prove you out" of your cynical view-points. But that does not change the fact that cynicism is at its core a debilitating and isolating vice against true healing and, eventually, forgiveness.

But I'm getting ahead of myself. Let's backtrack and nail down precisely what cynicism is. Because if you're like me, you know what the term refers to, but may not have an exact definition locked away in your brain. Fundamentally, cynicism is **an inclination to believe that people are motivated purely and solely by self-interest.**

I want to retract, or rather, refine what I said a few paragraphs ago about cynicism being towards something or someone. Under the definition given here, cynicism cannot be towards things. Cynicism is a skepticism of the human heart. You cannot be cynical towards inanimate objects because they do not comprise the human ability to seek their betterment ahead of or at the expense of someone else's. Most inanimate objects' sole purpose is to serve mankind, or at the very least, have been modified to accommodate us in our daily lives.

You can't be cynical of a sponge. Sure, you could be pessimistic about its ability to clean the pan you left out for three days after cooking pasta, which now has hardened chunks of sauce and shreds of penne caked onto it. But you can't rationally believe that a sponge will intentionally choose not to clean the pan because of its desire not to get dirty. The sponge has no say in the matter of what it will do or how much effort it will put in. Further, a sponge also can't choose to clean the pan solely because it benefits it in some way.

You can, however, be cynical of a sponge salesman, who tells you that the sponge he is selling soaks up to five hundred times its weight and magically dries in thirty seconds. This salesman needs to sell his sponges because doing so results in him getting paid, and getting paid allows him to eat, feed his family, and pay the rent. Because of this, even if the sponges he sells may not be the best in the world, up until the money is given, he will say they most definitely are, without question. At the end of the day, he now has money for dinner, while you are left with a sponge that starts falling apart after four uses.

Sponges don't have motivations. They don't have agendas. They can't be selfish or disloyal or self-seeking. Those fabulous characteristics are reserved solely for human beings. I would say all living things, but even animals don't have the awareness to know that specific actions chosen for their own safety or prosperity are at the expense of others. God has prescribed the virtue of a conscience for humanity, who was created in His image. As such, we have a deeply grounded inner notion of what is right and wrong, as well as how our actions not only affect us, but those around us.

* * *

I don't think I need to tell you why I'm cynical of certain aspects of Christianity. I believe I've made it pretty clear why I may have my reservations. Maybe you do too.

Cynicism and doubt are not too far apart, as unsatisfied doubt, or doubt answered with wrong or hurtful solutions, often results in a cynical disposition. However, while doubt has the potential to be a useful tool in building our faith, cynicism's only function is amplifying the damage. While doubt is a question posed, cynicism is a question answered, usually by the voice of our own pain.

We aren't born cynical of anything. We've all seen just how trusting babies and young children are. At that age, every person, whether a close family member or complete stranger in line at the grocery store, is a good person who only has the potential to be a friend. It is not until we have a negative experience with someone that we begin developing these pessimistic attitudes. And as these negative experiences stack, so does the intensity of our demeanor.

Any and all pessimism, skepticism, and cynicism of others are learned from either personal experience or the experiences of someone who has passed those judgments on to you. Interestingly, though we undoubtedly have many more positive experiences with people than negative ones, those positive encounters rarely have as much of an effect on us or leave as lasting of an impression.

The cynicism I have accrued from the last several years of my life has been primarily directed towards three main facets: The church as a whole, close friends and peers, and relationships. I'd bet that the majority of people's cynicism has to do with one or more of these same attributes. I believe a reason for this is that a shared characteristic between all three is that they all involve intimacy and vulnerability.

Vulnerability is the key that opens the gate to connection, and connection is what leads to love, growth, healing, and wholeness. However, there is an inherent risk in vulnerability, which I believe is the price required to acquire such gifts. Vulnerability also allows the chance for us to be hurt. Like a knight shedding his iron armor in enemy territory, being vulnerable is intentionally dropping our shields, lowering the steel gates to the castle of our heart, and allowing entry to those who seek admittance.

Vulnerability takes courage, as it allows access to our true selves, our authentic selves. It retains no false fronts or inaccurate personas. It displays your weaknesses just as broadly as your strengths. In order to achieve complete trust, you hand someone a knife, the blade pointed toward yourself, with the full awareness that if they so desired, they could thrust it right into you, knowing the exact spots that are most defenseless, where the blade will sink deepest.

We have all been vulnerable, and we have all had experiences where that vulnerability results in us lying in a pool of our own blood, alone, a knife wedged between our ribs. I have been that victim more times than I feel I deserve.

I have been stabbed by that knife at various moments throughout my life, the handle held by close friends, trusted mentors, and communities I had once considered family. And though I continually find in myself the strength to pull the knife out and heal my wound, it seems that each time, there remains a greater hesitancy to offer it again.

We have all trusted people holding the knife. We have all at one point or another had that trust betrayed. And we have all experienced the diminishing trust and increasing cynicism as a result of our hurt.

* * *

Ever since the last service I attended at my childhood church, my outlook on the church has been one of extensive distrust and, in many cases, somewhat of a disdain. It doesn't help that so many churches and church leaders have been and continue to be outed in the media on what seems like a regular basis for being, for lack of a better term, frauds. In my mind, those people aren't much different from some of the people I had to deal with in my own church. The damage was only dealt on a different scale.

Simply put, there were people who hid behind their faith, in some cases using it as an excuse for their lack of conviction or ability to take responsibility, in others as a weapon to attack and assert themselves above others. It wasn't only my church or even a handful of churches. Everywhere I looked, churches seemed to be steering more people away from God than toward Him.

Churches were being used as factories of conformity, and God's goodness was being distorted and expressed in so many ways conversely to how it should be, which is through love. In my mind, the people who went to church were there to push their own agendas and strong-arm people into bending to their idea of what Christianity is, or were simply too cowardly to stand on their own two feet.

Now, if I had taken the time to look past my pain, as I eventually did, I would quickly have realized how untrue that is. Yes, there are people who fit this conjured-up stereotype of mine, and I have had conflicts with them. But to allow the bad to extinguish all of the good that many churches and their members offer, as well as all of the people who are genuinely striving to live their lives through the love and freedom of God, is to rob myself of the acknowledgment that the church is not a lost cause, which is how I felt for a long time.

Do I still have these thoughts when it comes to church?

Yes. All the time. And I know I'm not alone.

At the heart of it, I know that the cynicism I feel towards an entire set of people based on my experiences with a much smaller group is nowhere near reliable. Of course, my feelings, like those of my friends and those worldwide who have left their churches, are not invalid. Those feelings are real, and legitimate. However, the cynicism most of us now harbor offers no better answer to our hurt.

Do I see myself ever actually becoming a regular church attender again? I honestly couldn't tell you. Funnily enough, at the time of writing this, I went to my first church service this past week in over two years for Christmas Eve. For someone who went to church three times a week for the first twenty years of my life, I felt like a fish out of water. I was nervous, never completely comfortable in my seat, and aware of my constant cynical inner voices.

The pastor seemed nice, but what was he hiding? What was going on behind the scenes? The singers were talented, but how deep was their faith in actuality? Was being a part of the worship team the only thing keeping them grounded in their faith? Everyone seemed so happy. There's no way it was all truly authentic. Surely they were all just playing the part, trying to silence the mountains of fear and doubt in their minds.

On and on these thoughts flew at me from all directions. The sad truth is, it was because my trust had been spent, dried up when it came to church. I hope that will change, and the trust I once had can be rebuilt. I know it can. But until it is, my energy can be best spent declining to entertain those cynical voices, because the only thing that will come from listening to them is further isolation and a hindrance to that forthcoming newfound trust.

I don't need to add much more regarding my cynicism toward friends and relationships. When you let yourself become vulnerable to people, you are allowing them the chance to hurt you, with the trust that they won't. But every one of us knows what it feels like for that trust to be broken. We have all been hurt by people we once called friends. And many of us are much less prone to opening up to people for a long time after meeting new people because we don't want to give them that chance.

Why? Because we feel that they don't deserve to have that kind of access into our hearts. They don't because someone else hurt us. Someone *else* did. Yet this new person is somehow responsible and therefore undeserving of us because of the inherent risk they present. The *possibility* that they could end up hurting us the same way. That cynicism offers us nothing but lonesomeness and solitude. Who then is the one who really loses?

Ever since the mess that was my attempt at cultivating a healthy relationship with a girl I liked, I have been sour towards the whole idea of relationships and dating. I still desire one, of course, but I simultaneously have a distaste for it. As if the thing I want is also the thorn in my side.

I can recall several instances over the last few years where people I know have gotten into relationships, and that cynical voice in my head reintroduces itself, telling me that the only reason they succeeded at something that I tried so hard to obtain but still failed at is that they somehow had to make compromises to get it.

Even now, I am sometimes conflicted by the thought that those in relationships, primarily young people, have built themselves up on faulty foundations and are doomed to fail. Why? I couldn't tell you, as cynicism is anything but rational. But I know where it comes from. And I know that many other people are in the same place. Cynicism tells us that we deserve to have these thoughts validated, while all that validation will do is steal our joy and peace.

Cynicism is the killer of joy because it convinces us that joy is fake. It is the killer of trust because it convinces us that vulnerability will always end in hurt. It inhibits us from fully experiencing God's goodness because it tells us that anything good comes with a catch.

Don't let cynicism rob you of all the blessings God wants to bring you. Your hurt is real. Your feelings are valid. But don't let your past define your future. Nothing behind us has to dictate what is ahead of us. God offers us complete freedom. All we have to do is let go of the chains holding us to the ground.

> **Untruth:** *Cynicism is Just the Truth*
> **Truth:** *Cynicism is Founded on True Feelings...*
> *But Removes God From the Equation*

18

A LONELY ROAD

We live in the most connected era of human history.

The internet has enabled everything we do to be shared, broadcast, and experienced virtually with others, no matter where or how far apart we are from each other. For hours and hours each day, we are engaging with others, mainly indirectly, through the technological abyss of social media.

We are posting, liking, and commenting. We are texting, tweeting, and snapping. We send instant emails, and we rarely make a decision or form an opinion before first gathering the collective perspective of the faceless followers on our screens.

On the flip side, rarely do we do something noteworthy in our life, whether getting a raise or a new car or eating an expensive-looking meal, without sharing it with others so they too can take part in the memory.

Yet, despite our "connectedness," our modern society is perhaps the most isolated it has ever been.

Loneliness is a concept foreign to no soul. In a world that seems to accept, and even at times romanticize the depression and anxiety that has become the norm in far too many lives, it can sometimes feel as if perhaps this is the way that life is intended, at least for you. And despite the glaring evidence that every single person experiences the effects of loneliness to some degree, we still somehow find ourselves believing the lie that we are in the minority. I place the blame partially on social media's "perfectionist" illusion, where the portrayal of unrealistic expectations and fantasy is by design.

But loneliness is a curable disease for which we are offered the antidote. It's the voices inside us that deceive us into believing the hole we have found ourselves in is simply too steep to climb out of. The hooks that embed themselves into the victims of loneliness are only given their foothold when we allow these voices to dictate our thoughts and actions.

* * *

During my sophomore year of college, I found myself at the precipice of such a place. In the span of a year, I experienced a tremendous amount of loss. The entire experience with the girl I liked had come to an abrupt stop, and through a series of unhealthy and hurtful conversations, we cut off communication all at once.

Simultaneously, I found myself at odds with two of my closest friends of nearly a decade, and despite attempts at salvaging the relationships, they too ended suddenly. These three people each held very distinct and equally vital roles in my circle of core relationships in my life, and in the blink of an eye, they were gone, like a rug being pulled out from under me.

Additionally, that November, my dog, whom I had grown up with for twelve years, passed away just as unex-pectedly, with no preceding illness or slow decline in health.

The rest of my family was out of town, and I had come home from college for the weekend to relieve our dog sitter and do some laundry. Within the span of twenty-four hours, noticing her worrying behavior and symptoms, I had to take her from her vet to the emergency ER, where in the middle of the night, I was finally informed that she had complete renal failure. By the time I got home, holding her in a blanket in my arms, I couldn't tell whether she was still alive or not, and the next morning, she was gone. Just like that.

Another huge and highly influential change during that year was of course the loss of my church, which I was born into and had been a staple in my life for nearly twenty years. Like I've said, not only was the church as an organization a central foundation in my life, but the people there constituted the majority of my close friend group, as well as a vast majority of my wider social circle. I had best friends at my church and many friends who maybe I wasn't as close to but who had become a constant in my life nonetheless. I would see these people every week, if not multiple times a week.

Whether we simply exchanged a greeting and goodbye when we saw each other or had grown to become really close, the church was full of people I *knew*. And they knew me. When I was around them, I wasn't a stranger. The church played a pivotal role in me finding my identity; over the years, a large part of that identity was in the church itself. It was a part of my DNA. So much of myself was in church that when I left, I had very little idea where I belonged.

This all transpired within twelve months. On top of that, I was in college, swimming in an ocean of new people and experiences. And for the most part, I was doing it alone. Up to that point, I had made a select number of "friends," who I really never got that close to. My film group, composed of only fifteen students at the time, was structured in many ways to become a family, and many of my classmates got close, and upon graduating, many still are.

I had gone into my freshman year excited at the potential of being able to make friends with some of them, and while I did get to know them, not much came of it. Looking back, and even in the midst of it, I was aware that I was in a space where I simply didn't have the bandwidth to put myself out there to make many friends. I was in the middle of a crazy amount of social and spiritual turmoil, which occupied most of my time and energy, and I couldn't offer myself to these potential new friends. I don't blame myself or think I failed in any way. I was doing the best I could to manage it.

But here I was, having just lost three of my closest friends, left my church and the majority of my life's social circle altogether, lost my childhood dog, been stuck in and then left a campus ministry that I felt I didn't belong in, and feeling like I had almost no friends. I had a few, including one or two that I had known my entire life, which was invaluable. But for the most part, everything else was gone. An empty page. A blank slate.

Yet it didn't feel like the exciting beginning of a new journey. It felt like years had been spent writing a story, only for the file to be deleted entirely. My story, who I was, and what I believed was tied almost exclusively to those parts of my life that I no longer had. The seeds that had been sown, the roots that had grown deep, were in soil that had now been tossed in the trash.

It felt like I was starting over, which I know wasn't true, as everything that happens in your past sets the stage for what's ahead of you. But even when you know that, it's hard not to feel like the time and energy spent on those relationships was for nothing. I felt like I was being left with so much less than what I deserved to have. And I know I'm not alone in this sentiment.

Most, if not all, people experience this at some point in their lives. For many, this can also happen during college, especially for those who go to school someplace far from where they grew up. But it happens at all stages of life.

When we're kids, we lose friends almost as quickly as we gain them. In the flurry of children trying to find out who they are, setting out on different paths of interests and hobbies, social groups are constantly changing, and friendships are always in flux. We go from one school to another as we change grades, so we never really have the time to plant roots that go too deep. Yet, even then, it can be hard when it's time to transition to the next stage of life.

When we are older, the friendships that we have held onto and nourished become much more valuable, as in many ways, they represent a sum of the time, energy, and attention put into them. There's a lot more to lose, a lot more of *you* in that person that you don't want to let go of. And when you do lose those relationships, which all of us have at some point, you feel… incomplete, as over the time you have invested in that person, or that group, or even that sport or hobby or skill, for as much as you have become a part of it, it has also become a part of you. So when it's gone, you no longer feel like you have the complete amount of *you* that you have spent the time accumulating.

You feel gypped. Conned out of something you put the time into and yet are still seemingly left empty-handed. And when you start to feel the effect of that void, loneliness begins knocking at your door.

* * *

Loneliness is rarely a result of physical distance. You can be surrounded by people all the time and still feel alone. That's because, at its core, loneliness is not about being around people. It is about being known by them. *Known.* It's an idea that is not only central to the human experience but is the epitome of everything God wants for us.

He wants to be known by us. He wants us to know that we are known deeply and intimately by Him. Thus, He has placed a deep, soul-level desire in every one of us to be known by others. When we experience being known by others, we are experiencing God.

We crave it. Most everything we do is tied in some way to our quest to be known, and most of our deepest wounds and pain are from a lack of feeling known. Yet, in this day and age, the intentionality required on both ends to truly be known is becoming sought less and less.

As the world gets more "busy," and people get more distracted by temporary and instant gratification, we settle for being *acknowledged* rather than being known. Likes and followers have become a temporary supplement for an intimate understanding of ourselves and those closest to us. We feel good when we feel like another person has taken an interest in us, at least enough to like our post. Because that person, upon seeing something we put out into the world, took the intentional step to show their approval.

Breadcrumbs.

We have succumbed to settling for breadcrumbs, the barren leftovers of a feast that we are promised, and have inherited by right. The world has convinced us that these breadcrumbs are the best we can get. The best we ever will get. And we believe it, because we don't see how there can be anything better. Though we have convinced ourselves that it is enough, we are dying from malnourishment.

This is no secret to anyone. Every day we see the effects,

clear as day and right in our faces. Depression rates are at an all-time high among all demographics, especially those in their twenties and younger. Anxiety is much the same. People are turning to all kinds of fixes for their problems. Drug and alcohol abuse is soaring. Suicide is becoming a term known personally by every household. The list goes on and on.

People are suffering from an invisible illness, but the effects are anything but. Our world verbally promotes unity when its actions only cement the belief that when push comes to shove, it's eat-or-be-eaten, and every man is for himself.

We see these effects everywhere we turn, yet, when we ourselves are battling the same voices, we are convinced that we are alone. Not only do we feel lonely because we feel alone, but we also feel alone in our loneliness. Because of this, we can feel like we are the problem, and our circumstances are a natural response to our own shortcomings.

This is just not true—none of it. We are **not** alone. Ever. And I'm not just talking about the loved ones and family members in our lives, which is itself a valuable truth. God makes it a point to emphasize over and over again the fact that He is with us. And not just "us" in a general, overarching way. He is with *you* specifically. Not in sentiment, but deliberately and willfully with you.

Here are just a select few verses that express His desire for us to know this:

- **Isaiah 41:10** - "Fear not, for I am with you; be not dismayed, for I am your God; I will strengthen you, I will help you, I will uphold you with my righteous right hand."
- **Matthew 28:20** - "…And behold, I am with you always, to the end of the age."

- **Joshua 1:5** - "No man shall be able to stand before you all the days of your life. Just as I was with Moses, so I will be with you. I will not leave you or forsake you."
- **1 John 4:13** - "By this we know that we abide in him and he in us, because he has given us of his Spirit."

There is so much to take from just these four verses alone, which are simply some of the ones that strictly spell out, word for word, that God is with us. An astounding amount of scriptures attest to Him always being with us, which is really a through-line of the entire Bible.

Something that strikes me about these specific verses is how in almost every single one, it doesn't just say that we are not alone and God is indeed with us but proceeds to tell us what God's presence enables us to do.

Because God is with us, we don't have to fear. Because God is with us, we are given the strength and courage to withstand any trial or confrontation with man. We are told that because we have God on our side, constantly in our presence, we are now *able* to do these things. Whether we choose to or not is up to us, but should we desire it, God wants us to know we are capable of it because we are not alone. With God, there is no reason to fear; we are not weak, but more powerful than any trial and tribulation against us.

He is omnipresent, meaning He is constantly present everywhere, yet His presence is not vague or thinly spread. Everywhere He is, His presence is intentional. He doesn't just "happen to be" in the places He is. He is there for a direct and specific reason. He is in every place, with everyone, at all times, and is yet specifically in all those places for the individual person and circumstance that requires His presence.

Untruth: *We Are Alone In Our Loneliness*
Truth: *We Are Never Truly Alone*

Everything we do and experience, both good and bad, easy and painful, is on a linear path that only goes forward. God created time with the intention of us being able to use it as a tool to sow, reap, and grow. When we find ourselves in those moments of loneliness or loss, we often feel like we are backtracking, losing ground or time, as if we are at a standstill in our life when we should be making leaps and bounds in our social, spiritual, or emotional lives.

But loneliness can be a gift. Not necessarily the feeling itself, but the opportunity it provides. For the better part of two years, I was in a state where I was most often on my own. I had my family, which holds a value that can never be understated, but I didn't have a consistent group of friends, peers, or like-minded people to go through life with. As I write this, I'm in much of the same position.

I know there are so many people in similar places, the majority even, whether or not they are actually physically alone. The loneliness is there. And while there are times when I still feel lonely, looking back on this most recent stage of my life, there are so many things God has gifted me to learn and see about Him, the world, and myself that I don't think I would have had I not been in the position I was.

Don't fall for the lie that the things that happen to you are coincidental. Every single thing not only happens for a reason but is being used by God. Wherever you are, no matter how you came to find yourself there, is a place that God can use for absolute good.

There is no place you can find yourself that is out of God's jurisdiction. If you take a moment to sit and *be* with God, He will show you why you are there and how you can move forward. We desire to be known, and no one will ever know you better, deeper, and more intimately than God does.

And He is never more than a heartbeat away.

PART V

ONWARD AND UPWARD

THE MILLION DOLLAR QUESTION

If you don't mind, I'd like to start this chapter with a story:

There once was a man (what a way to start a story, right?). This man considered himself to be a good person. He had a good job, a wife, two kids and, for the most part, considered himself quite happy.

Every day, instead of driving to work, he would walk since his office was only a few blocks from his house. They were tight on money at the moment, and saving on gas really made a difference. The route took him right through town every day, where he would pass many other people.

One day, his phone rings in his pocket on his way to work. It's his wife who tells him he forgot his wallet. The man stops frustratedly. He was going to buy lunch today. Oh well, he would be late for work if he went back, so he tells her that he won't need it.

A few blocks down the road, the man comes across an older gentleman sitting on the sidewalk with his dog, a can at his feet, holding a sign reading "Homeless. Hungry. God

Bless." As the man walks by, he awkwardly tries to avoid eye contact as the gentleman glances at him. "Sir. Help me out?"

The man slows and looks at him. "Sorry, left my wallet at home." He pats his pants to show that he isn't lying. The homeless gentleman gives a disappointed but under-standing nod. The man attempts a smile and keeps walking.

Several paces down, the man instinctively sticks a hand in his pocket and, to his surprise, feels a crumpled dollar bill. *Must have forgotten to take it out when it went through the wash last night*, he thinks. He doesn't pull it out, as he is still in eyesight of the homeless man. Besides, he'll need it to buy his lunch. He continues on.

That afternoon, the man goes with one of his coworkers to get lunch. On their way to their favorite sub shop, the man pulls the crumpled bill from his pocket. Without even unraveling it, he can clearly see the one dollar sign in the top left corner. He puts it back in his pocket angrily. "No worries, lunch is on me today.," his friend tells him.

After lunch, as they head back to their office, a teenage boy approaches the man, a broken skateboard in his hands. "Sir, I broke my board and can't get home. Can you spare some money for an Uber? I don't live far. It shouldn't be more than a five-dollar ride." The man shrugs. "Sorry, kid, I would, but I don't have it." The two continue back to work.

As the work day comes to an end, the man cleans his desk to go home. He reaches into his pocket and pulls out the crumpled bill. There, in the clarity of the overhead light, he notices that next to the one on the bill is a zero. Ten dollars. The man shakes his head. It looks like he could've helped that kid get home after all, and probably had enough for a sandwich too!

The man walks back through town on his way home. He soon comes across a woman sitting on a bench in front of a bicycle shop. Next to her, a bike is propped against the wall, its front wheel practically hanging off its spoke. The woman perks up as he gets closer. "Excuse me! Hi, sorry to do this to you, but I hit a pretty big rock down the road and busted my wheel up. The owner inside said he can replace it and put it on for me for ninety bucks, but I only have forty-four dollars." She shows him a twenty and two tens, plus four one-dollar bills. "I know it's a lot of money, but would you be able to spare forty-six dollars? I can pay back every penny as soon as I get home."

The man looks at her apologetically. "I'm sorry. I left my wallet at home and only have a few bucks, which I might need." The two bid farewell and the man continues home.

That night, the man gets his wallet. He pulls out the dollar bill from his pocket and begins to unfold it to slip it in with the rest of his money. As he does so, he freezes as he notices not one, but *two* zeros printed on the bill. One hundred dollars. The man is confused and, to be honest, slightly agitated at himself for not realizing sooner. He tries to remember how on earth a one hundred dollar bill ended up in his pocket. He doesn't remember ever having one. He could have helped that woman fix her bike. He hastily shoves the bill into his wallet.

The next day, the man once again makes his way to work. As he walks down the street, he hears a loud *screeeech* somewhere ahead of him, followed by a thunderous boom. His leisurely stroll turns into a light jog as he tries to see what happened. A block up, a two-car collision clogs the intersection.

Luckily, there is a hospital in town, and as a crowd begins to gather, paramedics arrive on scene. As the man watches, a mother and her young child are pulled from the closest car. Both are dazed and bruised but seem to be okay. Still, the paramedics insist they lie on stretchers and proceed to lead them to their ambulance.

The man watches as the woman screams and struggles, not wanting to go in the car. "Please, no! We don't have the money. Please. We can't afford it." The man is transfixed on the scene unraveling before him. Just that past year, he had been sent to the ER after being involved in a hit and run. While ending up being fine and only requiring some physical therapy, the hospital bill totaled several thousand dollars, which he had to take out of his retirement.

He feels for the mother and her child. But there's nothing he can do. After they are safely secured, and the ambulance drives away, the man continues to the office.

The man sits at his desk, still thinking about the mother and her daughter. He pulls out his wallet and takes out several dollar bills inside. As he shuffles through them, he finds the photo of himself, his wife, and his two daughters. He smiles.

As he begins to put the contents back in the wallet, he eyes the crumpled bill, still folded over on itself. He sighs and unravels it completely, and freezes. Three zeros. There are three zeros. He squints his eyes. How can there be three zeros? A thousand-dollar bill? Is that even a real thing?

He calls his friend over from a nearby desk. "Am I going crazy, or do you see three zeros on this?" The friend takes the bill, and his eyes go wide. "I've heard of these. A thousand-dollar bill. They exist; they're just super rare. Where'd you get it?" The man doesn't respond. He is at a loss.

The friend hands the bill back and returns to his desk, but comes back only moments later, a childish smile on his face. "Dude, you have to see this." They go to his computer, where on the screen is a bill identical to the man's. It is on an auction website.

The friend points lower on the page, where the going price for such a bill is listed. "Is that…"

.   .   .

"Yup. A million dollars."

* * *

Needless to say, this is not a true story. Trust me, I wish it were. The money part, not the car crash, broken bike, broken skateboard, and homeless person. It actually isn't even *my* fake story. It's my dad's. However, I did improve it quite a bit (if I do say so myself). Now, after all that, here's the question:

If you have a million dollars in your pocket, but don't *know* you have a million dollars in your pocket, do you really have a million dollars?

Since the very first encounter with the homeless man, our main character did, in fact, have a million dollars. He could have helped the homeless man bountifully, bought the teenager an Uber and a new skateboard, gotten the woman a completely new bike, and paid the mother and daughter's hospital bills in full and still have practically the entire amount left over.

But he didn't know he had that much. So he did nothing. It wasn't because he didn't want to, but because he thought he *couldn't*. So to answer the question, "Did he have a million dollars?" I would say no, not in any way that mattered or affected his life or the lives of anyone around him. He only had a million dollars once he knew he had a million dollars.

We are millionaires, each and every one of us. But our currency isn't money. It is the Holy Spirit. Everything we are, everything we can be, and everything we are capable of directly results from the Spirit's power in us, *God's* power directly inside us, on tap.

The Holy Spirit guides us, teaches us, empowers us, and so much more. The characteristics of the Holy Spirit are so numerous that He (yes, He. The Spirit is a variant of God Himself and is a living spiritual entity) has a multitude of different names given to Him over the course of biblical history. Here are just a handful of them:

Counselor. Comforter. Advocate. Breath of the Almighty. Revealer. Helper. Teacher. Spirit of Might. Spirit of Grace. Spirit of Glory. Spirit of Knowledge. Spirit of Truth.

Everything good is from God, and since the Spirit is God in us, everything good is from the Spirit, and everything good is attainable right within us.

Jesus played, and continues to play, a vital role in our lives and our faith, but God didn't want to stop there in His provisions for mankind. Once Jesus died, He was no longer here with us. Gone were the days when people could literally *walk* with Jesus and witness Him face to face.

Of course, this was by design, as God had in mind something better than someone to walk with us. He wanted someone to *be in us*. And believe it or not, our experience with the Holy Spirit is *better for us* than if Jesus were here in person.

Don't take my word for it. Take His.

In John 16, Jesus is with his disciples, discussing His imminent departure from this world. It is the night before His crucifixion, and He is taking the time to explain why He must go, and equipping His disciples for what the world will throw at them once He is gone. In verse 7, He makes quite an interesting remark: "But very truly I tell you, it is for your good that I am going away. Unless I go away, the Advocate will not come to you; but if I go, I will send him to you."

The Advocate, aka the Holy Spirit, will make His way to

them only if Jesus leaves. For that reason, Jesus says it is *for their good* that He leaves. Another translation has Jesus saying, "it is to your *advantage* that I go away…"

Imagine being with Jesus, *sitting* with the actual Son of God, and being told that it is better for Him to leave than to stay there and be with you in person. I'm not sure I would have believed Him. I doubt all of the disciples did initially. How could they? That statement sounds preposterous. What could be better than having Jesus right there with you?

Having the Holy Spirit inside you.

Just two chapters earlier, Jesus is telling His disciples about the Holy Spirit and what to expect when He comes. In verse 26, He explains, "But the Advocate, the Holy Spirit, whom the Father will send in my name, will teach you all things and will remind you of everything I have said to you."

The Spirit will teach them *all things* and remind them of *everything* Jesus has said. Every teaching, every lesson, every truth that Jesus preached and lived is reminded to us by the Holy Spirit. That is because He and Jesus are one and the same. They are different entities, but of the same cloth, different branches of the same tree. They are both God, and flow from God Himself.

Having Jesus, aka God the Man, living and breathing alongside you is in itself something utterly incredible. The Bible is a testament to just how many lives were transformed due to encounters with Jesus. But having the Holy Spirit living inside you, inside every one of us, consistently testifying to us what God wants us to know and building our knowledge and convictions is an entirely different beast. Jesus knew the value He offered to those around Him while He was alive, but also knew that the epitome of intimacy between God and man could only be achieved once He was gone and the Holy Spirit was sent to take His place.

This one element, the Holy Spirit, is perhaps the single most crucial aspect to the effectiveness of a church body, as well as the enrichment of a person's life, that if absent, will render so much of their practices ineffective and counter-productive. It can often serve as the deciding factor between healthy churches producing strong, inspired believers and ones stuck in a hamster wheel of religious interference.

We have access to the most direct, intimate translation of God, whom, upon developing a relationship with, can grant us knowledge, wisdom, and guidance beyond measure. Yet many of us don't know it. Even when we know of "The Holy Spirit," we have no idea just how much power there is at our fingertips.

We are millionaires, but because of our unintentional ignorance live our lives struggling to make ends meet. We wonder when God will finally show up and gift us the numerous blessings He has promised, revealing Himself to us and making His desires for us clear. But we miss the fact that the one who is able to fulfill those requests lives in us right this very second. All we have to do is ask.

> **Untruth:** *The Holy Spirit is Meant to Be A Mystery*
> **Truth:** *We Are Meant to Know the Holy Spirit Intimately*

* * *

Not everyone knows the Holy Spirit. Many know *of* Him, but to say they have a relationship with Him would be a major overstatement. The Spirit surrounds us, much like a corked bottle is surrounded by the ocean in which it floats.

We are always in His presence, as He is everywhere, in every fiber of all things. He is inescapable, as He is a foundational atom of every object and every being. Yet, at the same time, we can go our entire lives blind to His existence and true power.

No matter a person's ability, their true potential is found and unlocked through their understanding and utilization of the Holy Spirit. This is by God's design. He has carefully structured the dynamic between Him and us through Jesus and the Holy Spirit so that in order to fully experience God, we must seek to know and understand each depiction of Him in their own uniqueness and differences. In our current day, Jesus is no longer with us on Earth. We learn about God through the testimonies of His life, but history can only go so far in fulfilling God's desires for our complete unity with Him.

God does not exist solely in the past. If that were true, there would be little reason to dedicate our lives to His majesty. It would be like trying to live your life off one meal you had ten years ago. You can try to sustain yourself with a deep study of what food you ate and what nutrients you received from it, but unless you continue eating day after day, you won't last very long.

God's power is not only eternal, but constant. He does not intend for us to live our lives solely from the inspiration of the past. While the past plays an essential role in our understanding of who God is and what He has done, real relationship with Him is meant to happen now, in the present.

The Holy Spirit is the bridge between what we know of God through Jesus in the past and where God wants to lead us going forward into the future.

The Spirit is our ally, who helps us in times of uncertainty and confusion. He is our light when it is too dark to see, guiding us step by step and leading us to where God wants us to go. Without the Spirit, we may have knowledge of the foundational truths of God, but we will never be able to truly know what God wants from us day to day, hour to hour, moment to moment.

The Spirit leads each of us on our own individual paths, yet every path leads to God and His ultimate glory while simultaneously our complete fulfillment and satisfaction in Him. We are pushed and pulled by the Spirit to do and say certain things that otherwise we would never have thought to. We are given discernment to deal with our everyday circumstances and overcome the obstacles that come with them. And most importantly, we are constantly being fed the life-giving peace and joy that fills our souls and validates our connection to God as the supplier of every good thing.

The Holy Spirit is one-third of a trifecta of not only invaluable but necessary elements to a complete picture of God. Without any one part, be it the Father, the Son, or the Holy Spirit, we are missing out on such a tremendous amount of God that it would be impossible to ever gain a genuinely correct depiction of Him, nor receive the totality of life that God wants us to experience with Him during our time here on this earth.

Yet many people and churches spend almost all of their time seeking The Father and The Son, while the Spirit is often perceived as a loftier, more supernatural force that is in many ways less grounded in reality and better left as a mystery. What a shame that is, as the people who live in this unintentional ignorance of what the Spirit provides us will never know what it is that they are missing. But they will undoubtedly *feel* it.

*Untruth: The Holy Spirit is an Added Bonus to
Our Relationship with God*
Truth: *The Holy Spirit is a Necessity in Us
Knowing God Completely*

What the Spirit gives us in freedom can only be substituted with the opposite. We are only able to experience the amount of freedom that we believe we have. When we don't know how truly free we are in Christ, we only live our lives according to the degree to which we believe we have been granted. And without the Holy Spirit, who reminds us that we are *completely* free, with no strings attached, we put ourselves in boxes because we are afraid to encroach on land that isn't ours when in reality, God has given us all of it.

In my own life, I have seen the clear distinction between those living in the Spirit and those who have not yet crossed that threshold. The differences are staggering.

There are the people overwhelmed by the daily obstacles and fears that plague their minds and inner peace, and there are those who can navigate them while maintaining peace and stability. Some are in constant fear and insecurity of the future, and some, while still having no better idea of what the future holds, are grounded in the certainty that if they remain steadfast in the Spirit, where they are tomorrow, or next week, or ten years from now will be exactly where God wants them to be.

* * *

Several years ago, my mom had an exchange with a woman from our church regarding the Holy Spirit. Interestingly, it also had to do with guy-girl relationships and came about during a conversation regarding those issues. This woman was a mother of teenagers, and she and my mom were in a disagreement regarding the dynamics encouraged by our church regarding boundaries.

This woman had approached my mom because she had heard from someone else in our church that my mom was "okay with two twenty-five-year-olds going to get coffee together." Now, if such a situation sounds completely normal to you, that's because it is. But in a church environment like the one I grew up in, a situation like this was actually questionable.

Just to be clear. Two *twenty-five-year-olds*. By all accounts, grown adults. Just getting coffee together. At a coffee shop, full of other people. Of course, my mom responded that she believed such a scenario was completely fine and asked the woman what she thought.

The woman stood there in silence for a second, pondering her answer, before eventually asking in full sincerity, "Well, do they like each other?" Sure, if these two people like each other, the dynamic can be slightly different, but COME ON. It should make *no difference* regarding whether these two independent adults should be allowed to go get coffee together. Even having to throw around the idea of "allowing" these people, who should be making their own decisions, shows the mismanagement of such a dynamic.

This is what my mom told her, albeit a little more level-headed, adding that these two people are able to trust the Spirit to guide their thoughts and actions. Remarkably, this woman responded, "You can't just say to 'trust the Spirit.'"

Can't you? Really think about this. Can you not just "trust the Spirit?" Is that not exactly what the Spirit's role is in our lives, as the one who is there for us to be able to put all of our trust in for any situation?

I sympathize with this woman, as truthfully, very few

things in life are as worthy or fully capable of handling our trust as the Holy Spirit is. In fact, The Holy Spirit, being God, is the *only* being in existence who we can be one hundred percent confident in entrusting ourselves to. And, to be honest, just how much trust would actually be needed for two people in their twenties to go and get coffee together in a public place? I'm sure on the Holy Spirit's personal list of areas in which His power is required, such a situation is near the very bottom.

How spiritually and emotionally crippling must an environment be in which people aren't even trusted to go out in public together, where the risk of falling into some unarticulated sin is so low that only those with the absolute lowest amount of self-control or sense of integrity would possibly find themselves committing?

Because of such an environment's robust lack of trust in the Holy Spirit, the people denied the freedoms that they should be encouraged to experience are then only able to believe that if such precautions are being put in place, they must be a part of that lowest denominator, where every thought and action they make is in danger of being sinful, and as a result are far beyond the Spirit's ability to intercede.

Trust, in anything or anyone, takes time to develop. Sure, you can be told that someone is trustworthy. But real trust is only built from experience.

You trust someone with something small, and when they prove that your trust in them was not in vain, you feel comfortable trusting them with something more, something deeper, something that, should that trust be broken, will end up personally costing you a little more than what you trusted them with before. And as more and more of you is put on the line, that trust grows deeper, stronger, and more fruitful.

The same is true with the Spirit. The Bible tells us an innumerable amount of times just how trustworthy the Spirit is, all in the hope that we will be convinced to *just try it*. Trust the Spirit with something, anything, be it big or small. Because God knows that absolutely no trust placed in the Spirit will be in vain. Everything entrusted to the Spirit will be fruitful. And once you see that, you will never go back.

Obviously, the woman who was having this conversation with my mom had not yet taken that initial leap of entrusting herself to the Spirit. And she is not alone. Not by a long shot. Most people haven't yet taken that first step in seeing for themselves if the Spirit is what the Bible chalks Him up to be. They may believe it in a more general sense because it says so in the Bible, and if it's in the Bible it must be true. But do they believe it enough to risk allowing it to affect their lives? Because at that point, there are only three possibilities.

One, it will have a positive impact on their lives. Two, it will have a negative impact on their lives. Or three, it will have no impact on their lives. The "risk" is that only one of those options, the first one, affirms that what they have been told is the truth, while the other two simply show them that what they have put their belief in is all a ruse.

Of course, I put risk in quotations because we know there is no risk, and any interaction with the Spirit will ultimately result in a resounding positive effect. Yet, if you don't take that first step, how would you ever know?

Take that step.

One step of faith. And God, through the Holy Spirit, will empower each of the million steps you take thereafter.

> **Untruth:** *You Can't Just "Trust the Spirit"*
> **Truth:** *You Can't Afford* Not *To Trust the Spirit*

THE CHANCE TO SAY GOODBYE

Like most people, I don't remember much from when I was in preschool.

However, despite my lack of precise memories, I do remember one thing. I freaking loved it. So much so that on the very last day before my inevitable transition to the mysterious and daunting land of kindergarten, I was an absolute mess of tears and mucus.

There is a photo plastered on a page in one of my mom's many scrapbooks of five-year-old me sitting defeatedly right in the middle of the kiddy bridge on the playground, my tiny pale hands white-knuckling the rails on each side of me, crying in pure anguish as I watched my preschool crush walk out the gate, presumably marking the last time I would ever see her.

To say I didn't want to leave would be a gross under-statement. It wasn't simply that I didn't want to move to the next stage of my life. I couldn't even fathom that life existed beyond the youthful euphoria and adventure I had experi-enced during preschool.

I had built a life there. I had made friends I believed until that very moment would last forever. I had made memories, so many memories, that I couldn't imagine leaving to succumb to the sands of time.

I must have sat on that bridge for ages, soaking in what I knew were the very last moments at that school, hoping that perhaps I could will time to stand still and make them last forever. But all too soon, my mother's hand rested over mine, signaling that the moment had indeed continued to pass, and it was time to go.

We walked out the gate and to the car, where my mom buckled me into my car seat as I stared out at the playground, replaying in my mind all the different memories that had been created in that wood-chipped paradise. My eyes settled on the water fountain, which sparked an idea.

"Is it okay if I get one last drink of water from the fountain?"

I'm sure my mom was a mere second away from telling me that, unfortunately, the time had passed, and I couldn't go back. But, seeing the look on my face, she unbuckled me and trailed behind as I dashed back through the gate, onto the playground, and over to the fountain. I took my drink, which was probably more like four or five drinks.

Satisfied, I surveyed the yard and had another idea. "Is it okay if I slide down my favorite slide one last time?" At this point, I imagine my mom began to get the idea. She nodded, and to the slide I went.

That wasn't the end. Not even close. That afternoon, I managed to do pretty much every single thing I had ever enjoyed doing on that playground one final time. I swung on my favorite swing. I teetered on the teeter-totter. I slid down the slide. On and on I went, doing every single thing I could think of before I left, and wouldn't be able to do again. I was able to experience the things I loved and the things I would be leaving behind, soaking in the moments one last time. I was able to process the end of a chapter of my life.

I was able to say goodbye.

Closure is a luxury we often take for granted when offered to us. It literally helps us bring things to a close, whether it be a change or transition in our lives, a past hurt or wound, or even a longstanding open-ended situation that hasn't been fully resolved. It helps us come to terms with where we stand in the world and in our lives. It is a gift, and not everyone gets to experience it.

I never got to have a last day at my church. There was the last time I went. But I had no idea then that I would never be back, and it was never treated with the reverence that would have come if I had known I was saying goodbye forever. Most of the definitive decision-making happened while I was at college, when I simply decided I wasn't going to return. The distance helped make that transition more natural.

However, what it didn't afford me was the chance for real closure. There wasn't much time to process the transition until after it had already happened. All of my goodbyes were done looking back from a distance. I never got the chance to have those moments where I could remember and truly say goodbye to all the good times and memories I had before I was already gone. I never got to have a last drink from my favorite water fountain.

There are many moments when I find myself mad at the church. It's no mystery why. But just as often, I mourn the loss of the church I had grown up envisioning it was.

Everyone has an area of their life that played a heavy role in defining who they are. For some, it might be their middle or high school years; for others, the time spent on a sports team or participating in their favorite hobby. For me, it was my church. It was there that I not only discovered who I was, but learned who I wanted to be. And while that community was responsible for some of my deepest hurt and pain, it was also home to many of my most cherished memories.

I often think about what I would do if I had the chance to go back and properly say goodbye. If I were given the opportunity to relive and experience those core memories that I have held onto and will forever be remembered as the church at its best. I imagine I'd start with the camps. Boy, did we have a lot of them, each one offering its own unique treasures.

I'd go back to my first youth camp the summer before sixth grade, where I went to bed one night on the top bunk and woke up on the bottom, only to be informed that, in the middle of the night, I had rolled off my bed, fallen all the way down onto the cement floor, my mattress had fallen off and landed on top of me, and my counselor had thought I had been knocked unconscious, only to realize I hadn't even woken up, but had somehow slept through the whole thing.

I'd go back to my third year of youth camp, which happened to take place during my birthday week, when, during the camp's infamous water war, some of my favorite counselors had pulled me away from the battle, taken me to a giant pit of mud, and rolled me back in forth in it whilst singing me happy birthday.

I'd go back to our church's annual Family Camp, which my family had never missed for anything. I'd go back to the year I was in third grade when a group of my friends and I had discovered an abandoned fort made of tree branches and rocks out in the woods and had convinced ourselves it was the home of the Sasquatch.

The very next night, a few of our dads led us on an elaborate journey through the trees in the dark in search of the creature, to find that one of them had dressed up in a monster costume and hid in the fort as a surprise.

It terrified us, and sent me to tears, not because I was scared, but because I was devastated that our historic discovery ended up being a hoax. The hunt for Sasquatch became a yearly tradition, and as the original group grew older, we inherited the right to lead and come up with our own eerie tactics and surprises for the younger kids.

To complete my journey through the camps, I would return to perhaps my favorite, which was the Father-Son Camp. In reality, I would consider it more a Father-Father, Son-Son camp, as for the majority of the weekend, the dads would let their boys run wild with their friends while they kicked back in reclining chairs in the shade with the other dads pretty much all day.

I would relive the endless rounds of carpet ball, the late night s'mores roast around the fire singing worship songs, and the annual night hike up the mountain to the gigantic cross statue erected at the top. And, though a funny memory looking back, perhaps I wouldn't choose to re-experience the time I had ridden my bike as fast as I could down the hiking trail declining down a hill, only to have one of my best friends waiting at the bottom with his bike, which he pushed directly into my path, sending me careening forward over my handlebars and onto the grass.

I would go back to all of the Friday night youth group devotionals, which were a fond memory in their own right, but more specifically to relive the car rides there and back. Cars packed full of kids like sardines, talking, laughing, sometimes arguing, but always bonding through the unity of a shared life.

Youth group devotionals weren't merely events where

we met up once a week. They were part of an ongoing journey, one organized affair among the countless unorganized happenings of a life traversed with the people around you. In fact, I would argue that some of the places where Christ was seen and experienced most weren't even during church, but all the times in between.

Like the sleepovers. The many, many sleepovers hosted at my house, often weekly, sometimes even more. The sounds of childhood and friendship echoed through our hallways constantly to the point where it almost felt weird when it was quiet.

I couldn't possibly recall all of the times when my bedroom was crowded to a suffocating capacity with friends, finding whatever nook and cranny they could to claim their territory and sleep in. During one particularly packed sleepover, one of my shorter friends resorted to sleeping on the bottom shelf of my floor-to-ceiling bookshelf.

I'd absolutely revisit the time several years ago when one of my cousins was in town for business and, due to a booking error, received a free upgrade to the penthouse suite of the prestigious W Hotel in Hollywood. The room was the size of a house and, at that very time, had just been occupied by One Direction and used in a Blake Shelton music video. It was the real deal: glitz, glamor, and luxury to the max.

Being that my cousin was there for work and wouldn't even have the time to enjoy the room, he suggested I get some friends and bring them over to take full advantage of the once-in-a-lifetime opportunity.

So, of course, that's exactly what I did.

That day was our church's annual summer festival in the park, and I secretly invited a few close friends to this super amazing yet extremely confidential get-together afterward.

However, my mom had a different idea in mind and, by the end of the festival, had recruited a squad of boys so big we didn't even have the room in our cars to drive them all. We had to hire some extra parents to help escort everyone to the hotel.

I'll never forget walking through the lobby; our sweaty, dirty, basketball shorts and t-shirt-clad troop of middle schoolers scampering through a sea of high-class, cocktail-dressed guests. We definitely stood out. I even think one of us was carrying a basketball under his arm. I'm sure people were looking at us and wondering what the heck we were doing there. Little did they know, we were headed to the best room in the building.

I wouldn't dare miss the opportunity to go back to the day my family got the call that the adoption agency had two children looking for a home. After eight years of waiting and praying, our prayers had been answered, and it was time to add two to our family.

The call came during one of my baseball games, which just so happened to be against one of my best friends from church. His whole family was in the stands, and a third church family had come to support us both. When I left the field, they were all waiting together to tell me the news.

We got them that very night. It was a rare case where they needed to find a home immediately. And though we had been waiting for so many years, we were embarrassingly unprepared. We had a room set aside, but other than that, we had practically nothing.

As we made the drive to where we would pick them up, my mom shared the news with a few of our closest friends, and by the time we got home that night with my new baby brother and sister, only a few hours later, our front porch was almost entirely covered with childcare supplies, from diapers, to baby formula, to blankets and clothes, to toys, and even a bed.

Being part of a church community meant more than meeting a few times a week to share in our love for God. It was a family, people who were there to support you in your times of need and people to support in theirs. When you were a part of the church, you were never truly alone.

Each of these moments truly serve as glimpses into the church at its best, the times where God's presence shone like the sun and remains just as bright all these years later. But one thing I've learned is that the deepest, most mean- ingful moments can come amid the clouds and rain just as often as the blue skies. Those times may not be nearly as easy to live through, but are simultaneously some of the truest testaments to the power of unity in Christ.

I'd go back to when I was five and woke up unable to walk. I was in the hospital for a few days as I was treated for Toxic Synovitis. Funnily enough, I hardly remember how it felt, or much of my treatment or recovery at all. What I remember most was all the friends that came to visit, bringing get-well cards and balloons, treats, and knick- knacks to quench my boredom laying in the hospital bed all day. Nearly all the photos from my hospital stay are with the people who had come to see that I was okay.

I'd go back to the period in middle school when my two younger siblings weren't yet officially adopted but had been in our family for two years. There had been a sudden complication in their adoption process, and my parents were in court fighting to be able to keep them when it seemed very likely that they might be taken from us.

The process went on for weeks, and within that period of time our church family showed up in some truly unimag- inable ways. In total, seventy-four letters were written by different friends and peers to intercede for our family and persuade the judge that we were the best fit for these kids. On the day of the final hearing, the letters sat in a giant stack on his desk.

Additionally, the night before the final ruling, a prayer night was held at the home of our head pastor, where over sixty members of our church stuffed themselves into rooms and flooded the backyard, all engaged in intentional, interceding prayer for the judge's ruling to be in our favor.

And God heard all of them.

I'd go back to the day my parents, my two siblings, and I attended court the day the adoption was finalized. Just as our friends were with us in the battle, they were there to share in the victory. Several families showed up at the courthouse to celebrate the day, more than were allowed to actually be there.

I'd go back to when I was six, and a miscarriage led to a near-death incident that left my mom in the hospital for weeks, and on bed rest for three years. She was a stay-at-home mom and was the one most involved in my day-to-day life, taking me to school, planning my after-school activities, sports teams, meals, friends, and everything in between.

When she could no longer do any of that, my dad had to step in the best he could, but with his own job, there was no way he could manage everything in my life, be there for everything my mom needed, and keep us financially stable.

Thank God we had our church. I don't know how we would have gotten through it if we didn't. From meals to car rides to playdates after school when there was no one to pick me up and sleepovers when I needed to be out of the house, my family and I were supported immeasurably for those three years by the friends in our church. In many cases, friends may not even be the right word. They were family, and truly lived by the idea that we were a body.

When one part of the body is ill, it is the job of the parts that are well to assist it in getting everything it needs to get better. Because of our church, we were able to get better.

* * *

Being able to mourn is perhaps one of the most vital and valuable parts of going through a loss. It is the chance to express our grief, helping us preserve our memories and freeing us to move on to what God has waiting for us. Sometimes we think that grief and mourning only apply to the death and loss of loved ones, people, but in reality, we can experience grief in any aspect of our lives that holds deep meaning to us.

In mourning the loss of my church, I'm not just saying goodbye to the physical church that I've left. I'm saying goodbye to all of these moments, some small and fleeting, others continual and deep-rooted, that together create a quality that far exceeds a church's tangible structures. I believe that quality to be the authentic spirit of Christ, full of a love that surpasses all understanding, an inexpressible joy, a unity of heart and mind, and a hope that cannot be shaken.

God's church cannot be confined to four walls and a roof; it is lamentable that we even try to do so, as God is simply too big to fit. Church, true church, exists inside of us, as God lives inside us, in our hearts, our minds, and our souls. Church is not stagnant, but ever-evolving, ever-growing, ever-deepening, as the lives of those who seek it are being led into deeper intimacy with Christ.

I know that I am not truly leaving any of these moments behind. They will stay with me forever and will always be a reminder of what church can be, what it *should* be. But it just may be this exact notion that also allows me to see the disheartening reality that this is not what church always is.

I am not saying goodbye to church, and if it hasn't been clear, I am *definitely* not saying goodbye to God. What I'm saying goodbye to is the mistaken ideas of God that a church experience has led myself and many others to believe.

I am saying goodbye to the notion that church is a one-dimensional, un-evolving, and irreproachable construct. I am saying goodbye to a culture that invalidates and ostracizes those who don't conform to a specific mold and sacrifices the one for the ninety-nine. Most of all, I am saying goodbye to all of the shame, insecurity, and fear that has infiltrated and taken root in the hearts and minds of so many people, including myself, as a result of conforming to all of these spiritual misrepresentations.

Alexander Graham Bell, the man most widely known as the inventor of the telephone, has a quote that I am sure you are familiar with: "When God closes one door, He opens another." Everything in our lives has a beginning, and everything has an end. Every morning, the sun rises over the horizon, signaling the start of a new day, and every night, the sun sets, drawing that day to a close. Every sentence has a period. Every breath in has a breath out, just as every first breath at the start of a life is brought full circle with a final breath at the end.

I believe this to be one of God's most ingenious creations. Impermanence. Finiteness. Transiency. Which are all smart sounding words simply meaning that things don't last forever, not because they have failed to do so, but because they were built not to do so.

We were created and put in temporary bodies, on a temporary planet, with temporary life spans so that we would be able to distinguish the value in every fleeting moment. We are given not only a beginning and an end, but the *awareness* of that beginning and end, so that we can intentionally choose what we spend our time doing, our focus engaging, and our energy chasing. We cannot do everything because we simply haven't the time. So we must choose to spend our precious time doing what brings us joy, and hope, and love, and peace, and inspiration, and life. Often, this means having to move on from the things that don't.

Goodbyes are rarely easy, even when that which you are leaving behind is clearly better off that way. It is always difficult to leave what we know and step into what we don't. The unknown is a scary place, full of unquantifiable variables and incalculable risk. But when we remind ourselves that one door closing means that, somewhere, another is beginning to open, it suddenly becomes less about what we are saying goodbye to and more about that to which we are preparing to say hello.

We may not always be certain what awaits us on the other side of this new door, but one thing is most definitely assured. If the door was opened by God, what lies behind it is greater than anything we could possibly hope for or imagine.

Here's to the goodbyes. But more importantly...

Here's to the hellos.

TELL ME TO COME

If the last two years have taught me anything, it's that we truly have no idea what God's plans are for our lives. And I'm sure I'm not alone.

Halfway through my sophomore year at UCLA, I was in the midst of setting the foundation for the beginning of what I hoped would be a successful career in the film-making industry. I was narrowing down my desired focus for the remainder of my classes and studies, sending out resumes to some of the top studios in LA for internships, and was gearing up to finally put my knowledge to use and make a film.

But then came a little something called the Coronavirus, and that all kind of... stopped. Not for all of us in my class, and not all in the same way. Because while not having in-person classes definitely made a difference for all of us regarding being able to work on sets and make films, not having to actually be at UCLA opened up the possibility for me to make some decisions that drastically altered the trajectory in which I was heading.

I moved to Austin, Texas, and finished my classes online.

I left the heart of the filmmaking world and instead began to dig new roots out in Austin. Of course, I still want to make films and be a writer (duh), but the approach is already looking much different than what I had imagined two years ago. And it's not just my career path that is different. I had already left my church before I had decided to move to Texas, yet, even so, leaving the state entirely in many ways set the stage for a complete reset. Not only was I not going to my church anymore, but I wasn't even near any of the people I grew up with.

So much changed for me within these past two years, as it did for almost everybody in some form or fashion. Many people were forced to stop the day-to-day routine they were used to and were finally given the opportunity to think about where they were in their lives and what changes might be best for them.

Maybe that meant changing professions or hobbies. Perhaps it meant leaving or changing church ministries or schools. I know handfuls of people who did both of these things. We may think we know where our life is headed, but we can be proven wrong with the snap of a finger.

So what are we to do about it? There are really two options.

The first is that we can resist it, clambering and fighting tooth and nail to hold on to what we perceive to be the way our life should go, and in the end, still fail because we have no control over it anyway. Or, we can surrender, with the knowledge that we have no control, and thus we should give ourselves over completely to God, the one in total control.

I don't know about you, but the latter seems much more enjoyable to me. And here's the thing. People often assume that this way of living is much more stressful because we are constantly being thrown for loops we weren't anticipating, and we feel powerless over our own lives. But honestly, when has trying to keep control over our lives resulted in anything other than being thrown for unforeseen loops and an ultimate feeling of powerlessness?

That is where we start. That is already our ground zero. When we give it all over to God, we are also able to surrender those feelings and experiences. Believe me when I say that a life where all control has been surrendered to God is the most peaceful life you will ever live. He guarantees it. "Therefore, since we have been justified through faith, we have peace with God through our Lord Jesus Christ." (Romans 5:1)

Our faith in God's truths and promises is what justifies us and allows us to experience them. He promises us peace, along with a plethora of other incredible blessings. He tells us that if we truly believe in Him and allow ourselves to give up our control (or at least, our *perceived* control), He will take care of us and exchange that sense of control for peace and joy.

Sounds like a pretty good deal if you ask me. And unlike nearly every other trade deal in the history of mankind, this deal doesn't require that we do anything more than we already are. Rather, it asks us to do less, and let God do it for us.

This doesn't mean we should do nothing with our lives, however. That would be ludicrous, as God tells us that we were created intentionally because He has a plan for each of us; there are things that He desires for us to do during our time on earth to ultimately be able to experience Him fully and lead others to do the same so that He may be fully glorified and we may be fully satisfied. If we can't control our lives, how should we go about directing the path we take?

One step at a time.

* * *

You've heard of the story of Jesus walking on water, right? If not... yeah, He does that from time to time. Let's do a quick rehash. Jesus had just finished feeding five thousand people with five loaves of bread and two fish. Yup. He also does that. After everyone is full and happy, He tells His disciples to head out onto the lake for the opposite shore while He stays behind and prays.

The disciples head out, and after Jesus has His one on one time with His dad, He heads out to meet them on the water. Only, He doesn't use a boat. By this point, the disciples have been on the water for a while, and the boat is practically in the middle of the lake. In Matthew 14:25-33 it reads:

Shortly before dawn Jesus went out to them, walking on the lake. When the disciples saw him walking on the lake, they were terrified. "It's a ghost," they said, and cried out in fear. But Jesus immediately said to them: "Take courage! It is I. Don't be afraid." "Lord, if it's you," Peter replied, "tell me to come to you on the water." "Come," he said. Then Peter got down out of the boat, walked on the water and came toward Jesus. But when he saw the wind, he was afraid and, beginning to sink, cried out, "Lord, save me!" Immediately Jesus reached out his hand and caught him. "You of little faith," he said, "why did you doubt?" And when they climbed into the boat, the wind died down. Then those who were in the boat worshiped him, saying, "Truly you are the Son of God."

For those who have heard this story many times, we always remember that Peter walks on the water to Jesus, gets distracted, loses sight of Him, gets scared, and starts to sink. And while that in itself is a great lesson, I want to focus on another aspect that I find just as vital to the story.

Once Jesus affirms His identity to the disciples, Peter's

first response is for Jesus to tell him to come to Him on the water. He doesn't just jump over the side of the boat and start running to Him. No, even though, by that point, Jesus had confirmed right in front of their eyes that it was possible to do so. Plus, I don't think Peter was necessarily thrilled about the idea of getting out of the boat. A few verses earlier, it describes the weather, which consisted of heavy winds and huge waves. I don't know about you, but when I think of this story, I usually imagine Peter and Jesus walking on calm water, which in itself is a miracle.

Not the case. Violent waves, ghastly wind. The disciples were probably having a difficult enough time staying *in* the boat, much less thinking of getting out, which explains why they were so terrified at initially seeing Jesus walking to them on the water. It was probably insanely hard to see clearly through the storm, which is why they couldn't tell who it was. For all we know, they may have assumed they were all dead, which would explain why they thought Jesus was a ghost.

Regardless, Jesus tells the disciples who He is, probably yelling over the sound of the wind and the waves, and Peter yells back that, if it truly is Him, to tell him to come to Him on the water.

What came over him? If I had to guess, I'd say seeing the man you've been following around for such a long time suddenly walking on water in the middle of a storm would ignite some deep faith-filled inspiration. I'd say his request to Jesus was a gut instinct, ignited by the scene unfolding before his eyes. It was an unexplainable phenomenon, which sent a surge of Spirit-induced adrenaline coursing through his veins, and before he even knew what he was saying, he had asked Jesus to tell him to go out to join Him.

And that's what I want to point out. Peter had no idea what he was doing. The odds are, at that point in time, none of them did. They were probably freaking out, thinking they were going to die out there by themselves. But when Jesus appeared before them, that notion disappeared, as the way out was revealed. The way forward. But still, Peter doesn't move. Not until he knows what is desired of him. So he asks Jesus to tell him to come out to meet Him on the water. And Jesus does. It is at that moment in which Peter now knows that it is God's desire for him to get out of the boat and go to Jesus, so he does.

What do we do when we find ourselves in a state of unclarity, unsure of what we are supposed to be doing? We ask God to make it known to us and to give us the faith to hear what He says and obey.

Once Jesus told Peter to come, there was no hesitation. There were no additional questions. "Just to be clear, if I step over the side of this boat, I won't sink immediately and die?" There was no time for doubt. It was only once he was out there, when he let his focus drift from Jesus to the obstacles around him, that he began to sink. But when he was locked in to Jesus, every step was successful.

Have you ever thought about the fact that when Jesus tells Peter to come to Him on the water, He has no idea what will happen to him? Unfortunately, part of the deal of becoming fully human involves forfeiting your ability to see the future. Jesus was indeed fully human and therefore had no clue whether Peter, upon stepping out of the boat, would walk atop the water like Him or sink right through the surface. Furthermore, He didn't know that in mere seconds Peter would be struggling for his life after losing focus of Him and starting to drown.

Yet, for every detail Jesus didn't know, He was sure of one thing: He would be there with him. Jesus knew that what awaited Peter out on the water with Him was the next step he needed to take to have his faith elevated and for His own ultimate power and glory to be revealed. There were things that Peter needed to learn and that Jesus wanted to show him. But He could only do it if Peter met Him on the water. If he had the faith to do so, Jesus would be there to make sure he made it back safely.

We are all going to go through pain and suffering. Many of us have already accumulated the scars of innumerable past hurts and hardships. That won't stop, as adversity will always be a part of our future. But don't be discouraged by this fact or fall for the lie that adversity equals defeat. Obstacles are opportunities. Sure, it can be an opportunity for defeat if we allow it. But it is just as equally the opportunity for breakthrough.

Jesus knew that calling Peter out onto the waves would be the breakthrough he needed to show him just how important it was that he kept his focus on Him. But in order to show him that importance, He had to show him what it was like when he didn't. Yet, even in the moment of Peter's panic and faltering, Jesus doesn't let him drown. He grabs him and pulls him up.

We are never alone in our suffering. In every difficult situation, Jesus is holding out His hand for us to grab onto. If we do, He will pull us right back up with Him. But we have to look for it. When Peter was drowning, if he looked anywhere but up, he would not have seen Jesus' outstretched hand.

The same applies to us. We can look in many places, but if we aren't looking up, we won't see the hand. Our hardships are never meant to be our end, but are tools God uses to strengthen us and deepen our faith. His hope is that our assurance in that fact will trump our fear of getting out of the boat and meeting Him on the waves.

God is the only being who knows everything that will happen in your life, from the moment you are born to the moment you die. He is the only one with the whole picture. Why wouldn't He be the one you'd want directing your steps? When we wait on God to show us what He wants us to do, we are requiring ourselves to listen to the Holy Spirit to guide us rather than resting on our own flawed judgment, discernment, and desires.

Untruth: *You Have to Hold On, and Keep Control*
Over Your Life
Truth: *You Have to Let Go, and Step Out of*
the Boat

Don't buy into the lie that you have to have every step of your life planned out. What if you had nothing planned out, but instead were fully in tune with where the Spirit was leading you every day? You wouldn't be lost. You would be completely secure and confident in where you were and where you were going.

That's what God is offering us. In the middle of a turbulent world, He wants us to meet Him on the water. All He needs from us is the heart to ask Him to tell us to come.

KNOW WHAT YOU BELIEVE, AND KNOW WHAT YOU DON'T

Congratulations. You've made it to the end of the road. Whether it took you six months or an afternoon, you have read through this entire book and are almost done.

Why?

Don't misinterpret the question. What I'm *not* asking you is why on earth you would ever read something that I wrote. I have a little more self-esteem than that. What I'm asking is what your reason was for reading it. Why did you pick it up and start reading? And why have you decided to stick with it all the way through to the end?

I'll tell you what I think.

I think it's because you long for truth.

You are not alone in this. Everyone longs for truth. In fact, the search for truth is one of mankind's most significant and purposeful quests. In an age where the definition of truth is becoming increasingly ambiguous and obscure, our need for objective truth remains just as essential as ever.

This is because the presence and knowledge of truth produces meaning. If there is no truth, no absolute spine to the questions of the universe, then there is no meaning. And if there is no meaning, we have no purpose.

Everything we do is out of our desire and need for meaning. Everything from the intricacies of language and words to the monumentality of legacy and love is founded in, and proof of, the necessity for the things we do to mean something.

Truth is the source from which we are able to perceive our meaning. People spend their entire lives searching for truth, and if they end up not being able to *find* it, they resort to *fabricating* it. They don't think of it like that, convincing themselves that it is not fake but real. People coin the beliefs they have concocted out of their own subjective desires as being "their truth." Usually, the truths that end up being constructed are based on emotion rather than reason, feeling rather than intellect, heart rather than mind. This doesn't make those beliefs invalid, as what someone *feels* always comes from an inward place that is true. But it doesn't make it *truth*.

Just the other day, I was reading about the essence of truth, and one of the main ideas was that while there are many "true" things all around us, the truth that our souls long for is not informational, or centered around data or facts. The absolute truth that ultimately brings us complete satisfaction and fulfillment is relational. As such, truth is not something we conclude. It is something we become.

Real truth does not simply enlighten you. It transforms you. And throughout the entire history of human existence, while there have been multitudes of people who claim to know truth, there is only one who claims to *be* truth. I think we all know who that is.

Once we become aware of this notion, that perhaps the truth we seek so earnestly is found only through Jesus, the drive in our hearts to connect to, and thus attain, this truth leads us down the path to getting closer to Him.

Usually, at some point or another, this leads us to church. We find a community of people who claim that they can help show us why Jesus is in fact this truth. And many do. Many churches are able to lead others into attaining the truth that Jesus offers because they themselves are founded on these truths. Unfortunately, there are also many that have lost that purity of heart, that raw, unimpeded relational connection to Jesus that is required for the truth to be fully realized.

We don't know what we don't know until we do. Every single one of us, whether we have been Christians for fifty years or are being exposed to Jesus for the first time, have experienced that initial stage of knowing nothing except that we feel an inward inclination drawing us to Jesus. We surround ourselves with the people who tell us that they can turn that inclination into an authentic relationship and thus an understanding of the truth, and when it's true, that is exactly what we get.

But in far too many scenarios, though Jesus is plastered on the banner outside, His essence is only partially present. The truth He offers us has withered because the body of believers has compromised it in favor of other aspirations and agendas. Seekers come in search of the truth but are left with nothing but a jumble of crumpled papers, comprised of all of the ideas and beliefs they were told were truth, but turned out to be things that only pulled them away from what their souls were telling them was the direction in which that truth could be found—the direction of Jesus.

Untruth: *Truth is Subjective*
Truth: *Truth is Definitive*

* * *

If you grew up as a Christian, I'd bet you're familiar with one of the staples of 90's Christian children programming that is *VeggieTales*. If you aren't, well... it's a little hard to explain. All you need to know is that it involves a talking tomato and cucumber who teach young kids about God. (And we wonder why Christians can grow up to be so weird.)

There's a song that's sung on the show whose chorus has become a popular sentiment throughout Christian families and communities, exclaiming that "God is bigger than the Boogie Man."

God is bigger than the Boogie Man. When I was young and heard this, I always envisioned it as meaning that God was more powerful than any monster under my bed or fear in my mind. Which, to be fair, is what the song is saying. In the show, it is being sung to a young kid (an asparagus, in case you were wondering) who is scared in his room, and goes on to say that "He's bigger than Godzilla or the monster on tv."

But as I've grown up, my perception of this song has changed, primarily in my understanding of the Boogie Man. What if the Boogie Man wasn't just the monsters? What if he wasn't simply all of the bad and evil things that make us afraid? What if the most common form the Boogie Man can take is our own misinterpretations of God Himself?

Throughout this book, I've mentioned how small we end up making God when we resort to confining Him to a set of rules, ideas, and cultures. What if the Boogie Man is the accumulation of our own inaccurate, or simply incomplete ideas of who God is, all of the experiences that have left us with a picture of God that is smaller, weaker, and less able than He wishes us to know?

One thing I've learned over the last twenty-four years about humanity's relationship with God is that, while we preach and worship an all-including, all-inviting God, we often still like the idea of a God that creates barriers between those who know and obey Him the way we do and those who don't.

We like the idea of a God who validates our own beliefs, opinions, and perspectives, while condemning the faults and failures of others. Because it makes us feel good. It makes us feel valued. It makes us feel *right* in a world of so much wrong. But what we fail to realize is that everything God has done has been to erase those barriers, break down those walls, and instead build bridges over the rifts that we have created between ourselves. He knows that as long as we remain in our own bubble of understanding, we will never get an accurate picture of Him. He knows He is too big to cater to us alone.

We spend so much time looking outwardly, trying to identify and fortify ourselves against this Boogie Man, when it turns out that really, we're the ones who created him. Like Dr. Frankenstein and the Monster, we have created the very antagonist to God that we have spent our entire lives trying to rid ourselves of.

People are fleeing Christianity and church by the millions, and it is rarely because they got a good look at the real God and thought to themselves, "Eh, I could find better." The God these people are experiencing is nothing more than an apparition. The God we are giving them is simply an incarnation of our own beliefs, fears, and short-comings.

But God is bigger.

Bigger than our fears, for starters. Bigger than any monster under our bed or ghost in our closet. He is bigger than our doubts, uncertainties, and hesitations. He is bigger than our greatest missteps and largest regrets. He is not only bigger than all of our hurt, pain, and wounds, but also all of the hurt, pain, and wounds that we inflict on others, even when we proclaim to be doing it in His name.

God is bigger than every preconceived notion and inaccurate idea we have of Him. He is bigger than our losses and our grief. He is bigger than our goodbyes, as well as our hellos. Whatever the biggest, grandest, most magnificent picture we can conjure up in our heads of who God is, He is bigger still.

God is bigger than the Boogie Man, that is for sure. All He asks is that we allow Him to be.

* * *

In the end, it all boils down to knowing what you believe, and knowing what you don't.

It may seem like an oversimplification, but it's the truth, and the truth is rarely very complicated. We are all searching for truth, a truth that can only be found in Jesus, but all of the avenues we try to find it other than Him only leave us emptier and more desperate. Our world is full of people just trying to stay afloat, clinging to whatever they can find to stabilize themselves among the torrent of life's trials, problems, and hardships.

But God tells us we don't have to live that way. He gives us everything we need, from the truths and promises of His Word, to the teachings and sacrifice of Jesus setting us free from slavery to sin and the world, to the Holy Spirit, whose purpose is to continually lead us where God wants us to go and empower us with what it takes to be triumphant.

Yet many of us still stay treading, our heads barely above water. We can't find it in ourselves to fully take God at face value because we have learned time and time again that there is always a catch, and if it seems too good to be true, it probably is.

We have been burnt, betrayed, and in some cases, left behind by people in our lives who we thought were the ones who would always provide stability. But the truth is, they are just as lost as we are, and are simply trying to find their way just like us. As Christians, we preach the lifesaving truths of God to whoever will listen, but when we take the time to be introspective, we realize that so few of us actually know these truths to their fullest, most life-changing effect.

Life is a long hallway, with a locked door every three steps. Most people spend years at each door, trying desperately to open them, but end up running themselves dry because they don't have the keys. Knowing what we believe, developing our own convictions based on what God is saying to us, and developing a deep, authentic relationship with Him are those keys. The closer you grow to Christ, the more doors will start flying open as soon as you step up and knock.

Jesus tells us this exactly. "Ask and it will be given to you; seek and you will find; knock and the door will be opened to you. For everyone who asks receives; the one who seeks finds; and to the one who knocks, the door will be opened" (Matthew 7:7-8).

God is waiting patiently (though probably chomping at the bit) to give us all of the things we need and desire. Things that He knows He CAN give us, *easily*, should we only ask. But we can't ask for things we don't know are available, or at least don't believe are available to us.

That's the starting point. First base. Level one. We must seek God, knowing that when we seek, we will indeed find.

This isn't some elaborate game set up by God to keep you running in circles and jumping through hoops. We are not rats in a maze, scrambling into dead ends and constantly retracing our steps trying to find that sacred piece of cheese.

No.

The cheese is right in front of us. No maze. No tricks. We can smell it, even see it sometimes, but until God tells us that it is indeed as good as it looks and is ours for the taking for *free*, we don't reach out for it. Because we don't fully trust that it is precisely what God says it is.

One of the most bittersweet parts is that God won't force it upon us. He has given us every possible thing to help us see the riches available to us right this very second, for which the price has already been paid, but if we still refuse to see it, or simply don't accept it, He can't force us to.

How would you feel if the person you love the most in the entire world, be it a spouse, a best friend, a child, or even a pet, was dying of hunger, and you put a feast right in front of them, yet they still refused to eat, because they believed it was poison? Or perhaps they don't actually believe it's real at all. This is God's relationship with mankind. He is always with us, never spending a moment away from us and never ceasing to try to show us the feast right in front of our very eyes. Many do end up eating, and God rejoices every single time. But so many don't, and it breaks God's heart, over and over.

What's the point? Why does God care? Why go through so much for us?

For a chance.

"God did this so that they would seek him and

perhaps reach out for him and find him, though
he is not far from any one of us." (Acts 17:27)

All that God has done and is doing is on the off chance that, *perhaps*, we will seek Him and reach out for Him. It's a gamble, and God knows that in many cases, it won't end up going that way. Yet He persists, because any single person that manages to find Him, and thus find truth, and thus find life, makes it all worth it.

You make it worth it.

Because you are worth it to God.

This is what we know. It's what we *can* know. It's what God wants us to know. Everything else, every scripture, Bible story, parable, and church message is to help bring us to this good news. That God has a feast for us to enjoy, and we are completely undeserving, yet because God sent Jesus to die to satisfy the debt, we *can* enjoy it and, in doing so, enjoy Him. This is the Good News, and this is how simple the basis of our faith can be.

For everything it does well in helping people find God, Christianity has in many ways lost sight of the main point, and many of its members have resorted to knowing and adhering to Christian culture rather than Christ Himself.

So many people come in search of truth, the feast, and are instead fed substitutes. In the most serious of circumstances, they are even fed poison. Things that lead not to truth and life but to lies and death. Ideas that birth fear and complacency rather than genuine faith and courage.

Every person needs God. Many want Him. Yet a good number don't find Him because they are told what is being presented to them *is* God, but in actuality holds very little of Him at all.

As God watches, He sees all of the world's desperate souls, wandering, seeking, searching for the answer to their questions, the ailment to their afflictions. It breaks His heart to see so many get led down paths that are promised to lead to Him but instead lead away. He waits and waits for you, putting as many things in your path as possible to make you see the true way to Him, hoping that you will be able to differentiate Him from all of His faulty counterfeits.

His greatest desire is for you not to be tossed around by all of the different ideas and beliefs in the world, but to seek and know His truths and promises, to know *Him*, and for the road on which you travel to be straightened, your mindset and perspective of Him and the world around you to be simplified.

The way to experience God in His absolute fullness is by knowing what you believe, and knowing what you don't.

Know who God is, and who He isn't.

Know who Jesus is, and who He isn't.

Know who the Holy Spirit is, and who He isn't.

Know what true faith looks like, and what it doesn't.

Know what true grace looks like, and what it doesn't.

Know what true freedom looks like, and what it doesn't.

Know what true love looks like, and what it doesn't.

In 1 John 2:5-6 it says, "By this we may know that we are in him: whoever says he abides in him ought to walk in the same way in which he walked." If you know God's *full* truths and promises, you will be unstoppable. Contagious. And it will be impossible to stop the raw joy, peace, and love you experience from bleeding onto others.

So let it.

That is how you lead people to Christ. Not by instituting structures and practices out of fear or to control and condemn, but by being filled with assurance at what you are promised through Jesus and what you are capable of with the Holy Spirit. Jesus did not gain a legion of supporters by threatening them, or making them feel less than if they chose something other than Him. He told them who He was and what He could offer them. He loved them. And once they knew the truth, they just couldn't go back.

So walk. Walk in faith, not fear. Walk in confidence, not complacency. Be a mirror of Christ to others, not a distortion. Allow the freeing power of God's grace to transform how you view yourself and those around you. We are inheritors, "heirs of God and co-heirs with Christ," and are blessed with the privilege of being able to share in His glory. We are free, completely and utterly free, and because of this are able to experience God without bar or boundary.

How is it possible, after knowing such things, to settle for anything less? The only thing "less" is good for is wasting time. And time is much too valuable to waste. Don't spend any more of it unsure of the things God wants you to be assured of. You don't have to live your life toting a jumble of crumpled papers. The truths of God are definitive, His promises guaranteed. And because they are guaranteed...

We have no reason to fear.

> **Untruth**: *You Have to Have It All Figured Out*
> **Truth**: *You Can Trust God, Who Has It All*
> *Figured Out For You*

* * *

You sit at the desk of your mind.

Before you lies a blank piece of paper, on the likes of which a million ideas have before been written. Whatever you choose to memorialize in ink will be added to the collections of your unconscious, becoming one small fragment of who you are. It will affect every part of you, from how you think to how you act to how much of you God will be able to use for your good and His glory. A single idea may seem small, insignificant, but the implications are monumental. After all, was it not a single idea that got you here in the first place?

You pick up the pen and position it over the page.

What are you going to write?

AFTERWORD

When I started writing this book, I had no idea where I was going with it. Zero. Like I said on the very first page, all I had were a jumble of ideas causing havoc in my head. I wasn't even sure this book would be made, and if it did, what form it would take. Not until I actually started writing did the through line start to reveal itself to me.

The world is broken. This isn't news to anyone. But in this world, churches and Christians can be the light by which others are led to Jesus. That's what we are called to be. It is our God-given purpose. It is our destiny. Yet that hasn't always been what we experience. Often, all we end up being to people is further evidence that God is not the way to go.

So many people have been hurt by those who should be offering healing. And often, it's not because the people inflicting the damage are terrible or malicious. Usually, it is simply because they haven't found God in all His fullness. Only parts of Him. And the rest has been filled in by other means: fears, doubts, rules, agendas, even other people.

My own journey through these experiences has revealed

to me how not alone I am in them. Thus, the desire arose to lay down the truths that I believe people need to know about God, Jesus, the Church, and the Holy Spirit. I wanted to set the record straight on what I have found to be the real God. The *true* God. So that others, through finding Him, can take a look at their lives and let go of all of the parts of themselves that have been erected from false or merely partially true iterations of who God is, and who we are in Him.

I didn't realize how much I needed to hear it as well. I know it's a cliche for writers to say that the process of writing their book was therapy for them, but now, having gone through it, I gotta say it's true.

Interestingly enough, through writing out my thoughts and beliefs, I learned many things about them that I wasn't even aware of before starting. I believe my own faith is now more refined and directed than it was at the beginning of this journey (which is a nice way of saying that if no one ends up reading this book or everyone hates it, at least *I* got something out of it!).

Obviously, everything I wrote about are the things I already believe, but having to intentionally dissect and examine all of my beliefs so thoroughly only reaffirmed the truths I have come to understand about God. As the Mandalorian would say, "This is the way." It is. But if we are not careful of the convictions we are accumulating, we run the risk of planting roots in things that are not of God, but only replicating Him—feigning Christ. We don't have to live that way because we can know who God is in all His fullness.

I want to close everything out by thanking my parents. Amongst the constant noise, hurt, doubt, and confusion that I was navigating during these formative years, they were the quiet, peace, and stability. During the times when I found myself unsure of which direction to go, they were always there to shine a light and direct me. Most of the beliefs I now hold were grown from roots that they planted, many of my deepest convictions founded on their influence and teaching.

This is about uncovering truth amidst the lies. It is about finding our way after losing it. My parents always led me to truth and constantly showed me the way. Their love and inspiration bleeds through every page, every sentence, and every word of this book. I know for a fact that if it were not for them sowing into me the truths and promises of God and life, this book would never have existed in the first place.

There is so much noise in this world. So many different voices vying for our attention, sending us in so many different directions, most leaving us in places we never wanted to be. Thanks to my parents, I knew that in order to get to where I was truly meant to be, I only had to listen to three.

Mom, Dad, and God.

So thank you, Mom.
Thank you, Dad.
And thank you, God.

Made in the USA
Middletown, DE
20 September 2022

10745962R00182